So you want to
ADOPT... *Now What?*

SARA DORMON, PH.D.
WITH RUTH GRAHAM

Regal

From Gospel Light
Ventura, California, U.S.A.

Published by Regal Books
From Gospel Light
Ventura, California, U.S.A.

Regal Printed in the U.S.A.

Regal Books is a ministry of Gospel Light, a Christian publisher dedicated to serving the local church. We believe God's vision for Gospel Light is to provide church leaders with biblical, user-friendly materials that will help them evangelize, disciple and minister to children, youth and families.

It is our prayer that this Regal book will help you discover biblical truth for your own life and help you meet the needs of others. May God richly bless you.

For a free catalog of resources from Regal Books/Gospel Light, please call your Christian supplier or contact us at 1-800-4-GOSPEL *or* www.regalbooks.com.

Library of Congress Cataloging-in-Publication Data
Graham, Ruth Bell.
  So you want to adopt—now what? / Ruth Graham, Sara Dormon.
    p. cm.
  ISBN 0-8307-3899-1 (trade paper)
  1. Adoption. I. Dormon, Sara R. II. Title.
  HV875.G677 2006
  362.734—dc22   2006012603

1   2   3   4   5   6   7   8   9   10   /   10   09   08   07   06

Rights for publishing this book in other languages are contracted by Gospel Light Worldwide, the international nonprofit ministry of Gospel Light. Gospel Light Worldwide also provides publishing and technical assistance to international publishers dedicated to producing Sunday School and Vacation Bible School curricula and books in the languages of the world. For additional information, visit www.gospellightworldwide.org; write to Gospel Light Worldwide, P.O. Box 3875, Ventura, CA 93006; or send an e-mail to info@gospellightworldwide.org.

PRAISE...

So You Want to Adopt...

Each night, I hear fr
breaking dilemma; the
turn for information, l
warm and wonderful approach to helping people decide what
steps can be taken to ensure their unborn child will have the
best life possible. I have recommended it to hundreds of my
young listeners who did not know where to turn.

DELILAH
SYNDICATED NIGHTTIME RADIO PERSONALITY

As I travel throughout the country sharing my life story,
I tell about the beautiful blessing I received more than 40 years
ago when I adopted my son Fred. He has been a joy to me and
today is a loving son and a fabulous father. I am grateful that
my friend Ruth Graham has taken the time to tell her story,
research the regulations, and pave the way for potential
adoptive parents. *So You Want to Adopt . . . Now What?* answers
all the questions, exposes the emotional involvement, faces the
financial responsibilities, and delineates the long list of legal
regulations. After reading this book, you will have a clear
concept of what is involved so that you can fill your heart by
providing a forever home. I hope 40 years from now, you'll
be able to tell your story of your beautiful blessing!

FLORENCE LITTAUER
FOUNDER, THE CLASSEMINAR
SPEAKER AND AUTHOR, *SILVER BOXES* AND *PERSONALITY PLUS*

Many of my peers have struggled with infertility and considered adoption. From my experience with my adopted brother, I can offer them hope, as my love for him is equal to my blood sibling—some days I have even loved him more! But my experience is limited. *So You Want to Adopt . . . Now What?* offers a comprehensive look at the concerns and comforts that a person needs to be aware of when considering adoption.

MARITA LITTAUER
PRESIDENT, CLASSERVICES INC.
SPEAKER AND AUTHOR, *WIRED THAT WAY* AND *THE PRAYING WIVES CLUB*

Adoption is God's idea and I believe He is inviting more and more of us to embark on this adventure with Him. Every child needs to be wanted! Family is also God's idea. It's love's safe harbor for growth and development. Adoption is a clear reflection of what God, as our Father, has done for each of us. This book will touch your heart with God's plan for you to make a difference in the lives of children who need families.

TERRY MEEUWSEN
CO-HOST, THE 700 CLUB

We applaud Sara Dormon and Ruth Graham for their book, *So You Want to Adopt . . . Now What?* Adoption is near and dear to our family as we look at our blessing from China, little Sophie. We pray that many, many others take to heart the solid information and the gentle and loving nudge that this book offers. We join in the nudging as we encourage others to open their hearts and homes to a precious one in need. This we know . . . the blessing comes full circle!

CLAY AND RENEE CROSSE
DOVE AWARD WINNER
AUTHORS AND SPEAKERS

DEDICATION

*For all those who make it possible for a child
to have a "forever home."*

Contents

Foreword

Prior to 2004, Renee and I had never uttered the word "adoption," at least not in the context of *us* adopting a child. Yes, we knew of other families who had adopted children and we admired their kindness and courage. But we never for one moment thought it was for us. Besides, we were already blessed with two daughters, and we thought, *Adoption is more for those who can't have children, right?*

God didn't immediately place the idea of adoption on our hearts. At first, He began to challenge us in the area of overall compassion in our life. The place that I saw this missing was in our ministry. Yes, our speaking and writing (and my singing) ministry. I felt that Renee and I were very passionate about our message, but I questioned our level of compassion for those who attended our events. I felt that God was saying to me, "Do you really care about those people, or is this just a gig?" Ouch. This made me look very hard at the motivation behind our work. I wanted it to match God's will.

I talked with Renee about this and challenged her to pray about having more compassion for others. I sensed that deep compassion was lacking in her life as well as in mine.

When Clay approached me and told me that he felt I was lacking in the area of compassion, I was a bit offended at first. Pride, you know? I didn't want to hear his criticism. I felt that things were fine and that he might just need to take care of the weaknesses in his life and let me handle mine. Looking back, I can see that I was just being defensive and that Clay was simply telling me what God was telling him.

Soon after our talk, I began to have the strangest urge. I felt myself being pulled in a direction that I never would have dreamed. Mind you, it was a good direction, but one that I had never thought was a possibility for Clay and me.

I took Clay aside one day and told him about what was on my heart. I said, "Honey, I have been thinking and thinking about something. As hard as I try, I just can't seem to get it out of my head. It's crazy." I could tell that he was very curious about what was on my mind. I said, "Remember when you challenged me in the area of compassion? Well . . . I wasn't sure how to take that, but I have been praying, 'God, show me what that can look like in my life. Where do I need more compassion?'"

I went on to say, "Clay, I want to tell you a word—actually, it's a place. This is what I can't get out of my head. That word . . . that place is . . . China." Clay looked at me, still very curious. I told him, "I can't stop thinking about those baby girls in China."

Right then and there I knew what Renee was suggesting. Without her saying another word, I knew. My heart began to pound. I started to sweat. She was thinking—a lot, apparently—about us adopting one of those baby girls from China.

The practical side of me might have responded, "Honey, that's so sweet. It really is. You are amazing to think such a thought. But there's just no way. This just doesn't make sense for us right now. Our plate is way too full with other responsibilities. We already have two daughters that keep us more than hopping. And our ministry keeps us very busy with events on the road and producing various projects. Honey, we just can't." That's what the practical, safe and predictable side of me would have said. But that's not what came out of my mouth.

I was as surprised as Renee when I responded, "Yes . . . let's do it. How long does it take?" Renee, shocked at my response, told me that she didn't know much about the adoption process, but that she would start investigating. We stood there looking at each other, feeling that something new and exciting was about to begin.

Then my practical side *did* kick in. "So . . . how much does this kind of thing cost?" I asked.

I wasn't sure how Clay would react to all of this. I, as much or more than anyone, was fully aware of all of our responsibilities with church work, homeschooling, sports, music lessons, ministry events on the road and family time. We are like most families, stretched pretty thin at times. Don't get me wrong—we are very blessed with all of it. It's just that Clay could have easily greeted the idea of adding a new baby to our mix with, "Are you kidding?"

It was such a relief to know that Clay was open to talking about this. At the time, I didn't really know much to tell him about how long the adoption process would take or how expensive it would be. I just knew that I could not stop thinking about it. Clay's "yes" was the first of several confirmations that this was about to happen! We would see Chinese baby girls when we went out in public, and the stirring in our hearts would continue to grow.

Renee quickly began to do research on all that goes into an international adoption. What we found out is that it could take up to two years from the beginning planning stages to the day we would actually get our child. There is a large amount of paperwork and agency approval that must be handled. The time factor was a bit disappointing, because we were hoping that the process might go faster. Then, we found out that the costs of a Chinese adoption can run anywhere from $20,000 to $30,000.

I remember being overwhelmed by the number of things that had to be done to carry out an adoption. I was afraid that the financial strain alone would stop this plan in its tracks—$20,000 to $30,000 was a lot of money to come up with.

One night I prayed, "God, if You really want this to happen, You are going to have to slap me in the face with a sign." The very next day, that sign came. I took our dog, Moses, to the vet to have his stitches removed from a recent surgery. I was actually supposed to go the day before, but for some reason, I never got around to it. After the procedure with Moses, the doctor and I walked to the waiting area out front. From behind me I heard him say, "Ya'll are back!" When I looked up, I saw a family standing there and a woman holding—yes—a Chinese baby girl! I almost fell to my knees. I couldn't believe what I was seeing, of all places, there at the vet's office.

The doctor saw tears filling my eyes and said, "Yes, isn't it sweet. They just got back from China with their new baby girl!" He had no idea what I had prayed the day before. I asked the family if they had an animal there at the vet. They said that they didn't; they were just out making the rounds to see friends and show off their new blessing from China.

At that point, I just had to tell them all about my desire to adopt and my prayer the night before: "God, if You really want this to happen, You are going to have to slap me in the face with a sign." The lady turned to me and said, "Well it looks like you just got slapped!" We all laughed and celebrated together. Inside, I knew, without question, that God was telling me clearly to adopt a baby from China.

Renee called me from the car on the way home from the vet. She was crying tears of joy as she told me about the encounter. From that point forward, we moved full steam ahead through the paperwork and financial processes. We prayed hard, and watched as God provided for our needs! We aligned with a great adoption agency called America World. The agency was a wonderful ally in the long, patience-building process of international adoption. (We would encourage anyone with questions or interest about international adoption to contact our friends at America World at www.awaa.org.)

On December 5, 2005, little Sophie May Crosse was placed in our arms in the town of her birth, Chongqing, China. We arrived back home to America on December 15 and were greeted by family and friends.

Today, we just look at Sophie and shake our heads. How amazing! How unexpected from just a few years ago! From all the way across the other side of the planet, Gold blessed us with our newest daughter.

We applaud our friends Ruth Graham and Sara Dormon for taking on this amazing subject in this book, *So You Want to Adopt . . . Now What?* Having served with Ruth and Sara in various ministry events, we know that they have written this book with hearts of compassion and love. They really care!

When we began our adoption process, we had so many questions and concerns. We are thankful that this book will be an encouragement and a helpful resource for many, many families who are looking to adopt a child.

— Clay and Renee Crosse

Clay is a three-time Dove Award winner. He and his wife, Renee, founded HolyHomes Ministries, which encourages families to be set apart for God's glory. Clay and Renee reside with their three daughters in Memphis, Tennessee.

Acknowledgments

It takes a village to put a book together. We are indebted to those in our circle who have encouraged us, prayed for us and cheered us on. First, to Sara's husband, Bill, and her three sons, Billy, David and Peter, who have lived through many of the stories told in this book.

To our special ladies, Martha, Lyn, Jean and Flossie, who believe we can do anything and who faithfully pray for us.

We would like to acknowledge the contributions to this book that originally appeared in our book *I'm Pregnant . . . Now What?* Thanks especially to Windsor, Ruth's daughter, who has allowed us to tell her story over and over as we reach out to young women who have unplanned pregnancies (see chapters 5 and 9).

Thanks also to Joy, Cherie and Mary, who have also shared their stories and their hearts once again in this new book (see chapters 5, 9 and 12) along with Joy's father, Brown, who has once again provided the unique perspective of a birth grandfather (see chapter 12). To Debra Fox, Esq., thank you for writing the legal advice that appears in chapter 6. Thank you, Kevin Gallagher, for freely sharing again (chapter 10) what it is like to be an adoptive father. And thank you Matt Van Kirk for writing especially for this book your experiences of "growing up adopted" (chapter 11). All of your generosity and openness with your stories—and your hard-won expertise—provide inspiration to us and to many others.

Ruth and I acknowledge our own lasting friendship and we thank each other for our deepening respect and growing ministry.

Thanks to the members of the Regal team, who have believed in this project from the first mention of it. To Bill Greig, Publisher; Kim Bangs, Acquisitions Editor; Deena Davis, Managing Editor; Rob Williams, Art Director, and David Griffing, Designer—our hats are off to you for seeing it to completion. Special thanks to Kathy Deering, editor extraordinaire, who took a very rough manuscript and polished it for us. We have grateful hearts to all of you.

The motto of Regal Books is "To Know Christ and to Make Him Known." The team has fulfilled their motto and enabled us to get our message of hope out to those of you who are confronted with the life-altering issues of unplanned pregnancy, infertility and adoption. We pray that through your own experience, you will sense the faithfulness of God's love and grace to you personally.

Introduction

SARA

About four years ago, a friend of mine with a nationally syndicated nightly radio show, Delilah, talked with me about three siblings for whom I had been trying to find an adoptive "forever home." We were getting near the Thanksgiving holiday, and she felt strongly that we needed to try harder to provide these children with a home. Later in the week while I was watching television, she called me—right while she was doing a live radio show that was being broadcast on more than 300 stations across the country. She said, "I want to do a one-minute interview with you to put on the radio so we can find someone to adopt these children and give them a forever home." I was more than happy to comply, and off we went.

We ended the interview with her saying that if anyone out there was interested in adopting these three children, they should call my toll-free phone number, which she then gave out. She told me that the interview would be on the air at 9:00 P.M. my time, so I went back to watching my television show. Now, somewhere in the back of my mind, I must have thought that some special individual would hear this interview, make a call, and another forever family would be formed. But I never imagined that there would be 10 to 12 *million* people listening to the story and that an amazing number of those people would be writing down my toll-free number. Well, you probably already know the rest. At 9:01 P.M. my phone started to ring, and it didn't slow down for two days and more than 900 calls later. For six straight hours, I did nothing but go "click" from one call to the next.

Initially, I wasn't sure what these people wanted or expected from me, but I did my best to answer their questions. As time passed and the hundreds of calls continued, a pattern began to appear. These individuals had heard Delilah interview me about needing to find a home for three young siblings and knew that we wanted to try to have this done by the holidays. Because Delilah herself is the mother of adopted children, she has a soft spot for these children. Consequently, she was willing to use her far-reaching influence to try to help them. The people calling my toll-free number were loyal listeners of her show, so I realized that many of them were probably responding to her and not to the real need for these children to be adopted.

At the same time, I found out in a very real and tangible way that there are a lot of people out there who would be willing to adopt a child but have absolutely no idea what that means or how to go about it. They thought that all they needed was a desire to adopt and a nice home. After all, we see how pets are put up for adoption. We hear about towns that adopt other towns and countries that adopt other countries. Your service organization can adopt a section of highway to keep the litter picked up. The word is used so often and so diversely that its true meaning has been lost. After I explained to these individuals the details of what adopting a child would mean from an emotional and financial standpoint, many callers said thank you and moved on. However, many of them did sincerely want to adopt a child.

For all of you who would like to open your hearts and home to a child but have little or no knowledge of the emotions and issues involved in making this dream a reality, this book is written for you. We hope that it will offer you direction, encouragement, useful information and an impetus to provide a forever home for a child out there. This book is intended to provide you with a look at adoption from the standpoint of all the people involved in the process from the birthmother to the lawyer to the adoptive parents. We have even included the reflections and memories of an adult adoptee. To completely cover the range of issues and emotions involved in the adoption process would require an encyclopedic tome, but we have taken our experience and have tried to make it useful.

One of the best ways to navigate the rough waters of the adoption process is to obtain some insight into the mind, heart and emotions of all of the parties involved in an adoption, which includes the birthmother, her parents, the birthfather, and others who have gone before and have successfully fulfilled their desire to have a family through adoption. This book is intended to give you a look through that window and thereby help you to better understand what you need to do to successfully complete an adoption yourself.

By the way, we did find a forever home for all three of those children—in Switzerland.

RUTH

I am asked often how many children and grandchildren I have. I reply with a smile, "Three grown children, three grandchildren and one stepgrandchild." (I say this, even though I do not like the term "step," because to me it seems to imply some sort of difference, a sort of "lesser than." My son-in-law's son is definitely a full part of our family.)

Some people press for information about my grandchildren: How old are they? Where do they live? I am then put in the position of explaining that my first grandchild is one I hold in my heart, not in my arms. She was courageously released for adoption by my then 17-year-old daughter.

My contribution to this book is to shed some light on the young woman facing the decision to release her child for adoption. This is the other side of adoption, the forgotten side. I speak as an advocate for the birthmother.

So often in the adoptive process, the focus is on the adoptive parents. They are applauded and supported. And they should be. But off in the shadows is a young woman with an empty womb, empty arms and empty heart. Too often she is forgotten—invisible.

As I travel and speak to groups, telling part of this story, many people come up to me and thank me for talking about the courage of birthmothers. They say, "We never really thought about that side of it." That makes me sad. The birthmother is the very person who will enable you to receive the one thing that you as a couple desire most in the world.

Often this birthmother is gossiped about, condemned, criticized and ostracized. There is little support for her. Those around her expect her to go back to "normal" and just pick up where she left off. But for her, there is now a new normal, which includes a permanent hole in her heart. She may well be still in high school, but she is neither an adult nor a teenager. Where does she fit in?

I want people to see birthmothers as courageous. Yes, they made a bad choice and they must bear the consequences, but they also chose life for their child and now are willing to do a very courageous thing—release that child. Jesus said there was no greater love but that a man lay down his life for his friends (see John 15:13).

The birthmother of your child deserves your respect, gratitude and prayers.

CHAPTER 1

The Heartbreak of Infertility

Sing, O barren woman, you who never bore a child; burst into song, shout for joy, you who were never in labor; because more are the children of the desolate woman than of her who has a husband.

ISAIAH 54:1

SARA

If you have picked up this book, chances are that you are either interested in adoption or you know someone who is. If it is you who is interested, there are two possible reasons for your interest: you are dealing with infertility, or God has placed a call on your heart to open your home to a child. Either way, adoption should be something that God has called you to do, not merely a means to the end of having a family.

The purpose of this chapter is to deal with the first reason, the issue of infertility (the inability to carry a pregnancy to term), and to discuss it from an emotional and psychological perspective.

If you are dealing with infertility, by this point your emotions have probably been battered and beaten, your body has been subjected to things that you would never have dreamed would happen, and your spirit has been bruised—maybe even bloodied. We want to help you heal those wounds, while at the same time offer you guidance and encouragement on your journey to become parents.

It is probably safe to assume that if you want to get pregnant and haven't been able to do so, you already have researched the topic to death. The Internet is filled with website after website on treatments, books and techniques for dealing with infertility. Very few of these websites, however, deal with the devastating emotional toll that infertility can take on a couple. It is important that you as a couple receive professional counseling to deal with the issue of your infertility.

You may think that by the time you have decided to institute an adoption plan, the issue of infertility will finally be behind you, but that may not be true. Make sure it's behind you. We feel that it is very important to make a serious effort to begin the process to heal the pain and loss of infertility *before* getting on what could be another roller coaster of emotion. The pain of infertility may never completely go away. But when you hold a newborn baby in your arms or hear the laughter of a child who calls you "Mom" and "Dad," the pain will diminish considerably.

Infertility can take a huge toll on a marriage relationship. You and your spouse will need to deal with the sense of loss and go through the grieving process in order for each of you to be able to move forward into the adoption process. You may have spent so much time and energy on trying to conceive and carry to term that when you realize that this dream is not meant to be, you rush into the next best thing, adoption. I worked with one couple who spent tens of thousands of dollars on infertility treatments, but when the time came and they were actually chosen by a birthmother, they realized that they could not afford the adoption. Fortunately, they did get pregnant and had one healthy, biological child.

Who's at Fault?

It is generally assumed that infertility is caused by problems in the female reproductive system. However, research has shown that one-third of infertility cases are caused by problems in the female reproductive system, one-third are caused by problems in the male reproductive system, and one-third are caused by a combination of both or from other unknown causes. In today's society, one in seven couples struggles with infertility.[1]

Contributing factors to female infertility include ovulatory problems, cervical problems, pelvic and tubal factors, and uterine factors. Male-related causes of infertility include low sperm count, abnormal sperm shape, and low sperm motility. Today, the trend for couples to wait to get married and to start their careers before they start a family is often another contributing factor to infertility, because as each year passes, the chances of getting pregnant steadily decrease. By age 40, the couple's chance for conception is about 5 percent.[2]

Of course, all of the statistics do little to alleviate the pain and grief experienced by couples who want a child but are unable to have one. However, there are organizations whose sole purpose is to help couples deal with this grief and loss. One such organization is *Resolve,* which provides excellent services and support on a national basis (see the Resources section at the end of this book for contact information).

Keep in mind that while the woman in the relationship generally gets all of the attention, there is also a man involved, and he, too, can struggle with feelings of helplessness and hurt. Men tend to be less verbal about most emotional issues, and something that is this personal (especially if the infertility problem is caused by him) will be even more difficult for him to talk about. An organization like *Resolve* can be the perfect forum for men dealing with infertility issues to receive the help they need. Again, we must emphasize that it is vitally important for both the man and the woman in the relationship to address the issue of infertility before they move on to adoption or any other means of creating a family.

Know the Stressors
We live in a society in which most people expect to get married, have careers and start a family, although not necessarily in that order. Most young women today don't want to entertain the question of what they will do if they can't have children, unless they have been given a medical reason to do so. When the reality of their situation comes crashing down on them, they are often unprepared for the incredible sense of loss, pain and anger they experience. They feel incompetent, inadequate and generally useless. *After all,* they reason, *if a 14-year-old can get pregnant the first time she has sex, what is wrong with me? I was created by God to be fruitful and multiply, and I can't do it!*

A friend who experienced infertility said that when she was childless, she was jealous of every woman with a child or expecting a child—or even those women whom she thought might be pregnant. Baby showers became off-limits. Happy mothers walking through the mall were the enemy.

Although there is no set way to deal with the emotional stress caused by infertility, there are some things that you can do to make your situation somewhat easier. First, you need to know what stressors set you off, how you react to them, and how to deal with them. Some possible stressors include:

- seeing friends getting pregnant
- being invited to baby showers
- seeing babies everywhere you turn
- seeing unmarried pregnant teenagers
- viewing commercials and ads with babies or children
- thinking you are pregnant, and then getting your period

These are just a few of the things that life can throw at you. In particular, if you are dealing with infertility, it will seem as though everyone you know and everyone you see is pregnant. This is especially difficult if someone close to you is pregnant, as you will be expected to be happy for that person, not feeling sorry for yourself. However, as you become more aware of these stressors, you will be better able to deal with the emotions that they will cause.

Many years ago, I had a miscarriage. It was a very painful time for me. Those of you who have experienced this know that you want very much to get pregnant again, but you are afraid to try for fear of losing another baby. I was dealing with the loss in the best way I could when a friend of mine called to tell me that she was pregnant. The problem wasn't just that she was pregnant, but that she really didn't want to be. This was her fourth child, and I was still working on number one. It didn't seem fair. Later, my friend told me how badly she felt knowing how much I wanted to be pregnant and how much she didn't want to be.

The Emotional Roller Coaster

Another major issue with infertility is dealing with the emotional roller-coaster ride that often accompanies fertility treatments. Knowing when enough is enough and dealing with the uncertainty of the outcome of the treatments will be important aspects of maintaining your emotional and mental health. It will also be important for you to learn to take care of yourself and have a good support system around you.

Many of the emotions that you will feel during this time will be initiated by the hormones that you will take in order to increase your chances of getting pregnant. This, coupled with the feeling of being out of control and inadequate, will leave you feeling emotionally vulnerable. You will need to protect yourself while going through these fertility treatments and make sure your husband knows how you feel (even though he probably won't understand).

As impossible as this may seem, try to reach outside of yourself and realize all of the things that you are able to do for now because you do not have children. There are seasons in life, and for now yours is an unfettered one. Allow God to use you in the present. The best way to help alleviate your pain is to try to help others alleviate their pain. As Isaiah 54:1-2 states, "Sing, O barren woman, you who never bore a child . . . enlarge the place of your tent, stretch your tent curtains wide, do not hold back; lengthen your cords, strengthen your stakes."

Here are some other ideas that can be helpful when dealing with infertility:

- Ask those in your support network to read about infertility and educate themselves. This will lead to them being more sensitive and supportive.
- Allow yourself to be angry and express your anger (appropriately), through tears, yelling or whatever works for you.

- Allow your spouse to deal with the issue in his or her own way, even when it is different from your way.
- Don't spend every waking moment talking about it. Limit your time to no more than 30 minutes a day.
- Recognize that people don't read minds, so you must tell them what you need and how they can help you.
- Reduce uncertainty (a main stressor) by becoming as informed as possible about your particular situation.

You may need to give yourself permission to hurt, cry, be angry and not go to what will seem like a never-ending parade of children's birthday parties and baby showers. Although you can't live in a bubble—you *will* have to deal with friends or relatives who are pregnant—you do not have to pretend that your inability to have children is alright and that it doesn't hurt. It does hurt, and that is okay!

Sometimes, you may wish that people would say something to you to show you they care, but when they open their mouths, you wish that they had just kept quiet. Realize that people will often say stupid things to you. They will not mean for their comments to hurt you, but they will. There are certain situations in life that people really don't know how to handle, such as death, miscarriage, infidelity, unplanned pregnancy and infertility. You need to give people the benefit of the doubt. Resist the urge to hurt them back. Try to remember that while stress does not cause infertility, infertility does cause stress.

Is Adoption Consumer-Friendly?

Generally, women are the ones who initiate the process of adoption once the prospect of having biological children has been ruled out. A study done by the Urban Institute in Washington, D.C., found that in 2002, the interest in adoption among women aged 18 to 44 rose 38 percent. However, the number of women who actually took steps to adopt was only 10 percent (as opposed to 16 percent in 1995). This suggests that adoption needs to be more consumer-friendly.

Of those women who actually took steps to adopt, 73 percent already had children, 66 percent were married, and 27 percent were single. There was no indication as to whether the 73 percent who had children were experiencing secondary infertility or simply wanted to add to their families.[3] (As for the 27 percent who were single, we believe that God's intention is for children to have both a mother and a father. However, we would advise singles who wish to adopt to get counseling and direction from their church pastor.)

The Uncharted Territory

Before you pick up the banner of adoption, you need to realize that there will be a whole new set of stressors that will accompany the process. As with infertility, adoption is a situation that you have little to no control over. You do what is required of you to be eligible for adoption, you tell everyone you know that you want to adopt, you talk to agencies and to people who have adopted, and you read everything you can find on the subject. Then you sit back and wait. That's all you can do for a while—just wait for that elusive moment when some young pregnant woman looks at your profile and says, "They are the ones."

If you have experienced the emotional ride of infertility, you will find that the emotions involved in adoption, while every bit as unnerving, present a different set of challenges. When dealing with infertility, you at least feel as though you have some control, but you have absolutely no guarantee of a child. In the process of adoption, you have little to no control over the results, but you can rest in the knowledge that if God has called you to adopt, you *will* have a child at the end of the process.

Before you enter into the uncharted territory called adoption, you need to be as sure as you can as to *why* you want to adopt and what your expectations are. Otherwise, you might be setting yourself up for further pain and heartache. You also need to be sure that God has called you to adopt a child and that you are not doing it in order to feel complete as a person.

RUTH

As you wait to receive that long-awaited phone call, remember that there is a young woman and her family who will be struggling with her decision. She so desperately wants to make the right decision for the baby. She wants things to go back to normal—the way they were before. But just as when you bring the baby home, life will never be the same for her and her family. Nothing will ever be the same again.

Usually, the birthmother is young and scared. She is making adult decisions, yet in so many ways she is still a child. Her emotions are all over the map. Everyone is tired—very tired. And still they have to keep remembering what is best for the baby. Perhaps you are not all that interested in the birthmother's story—you just want her baby so that you can go home to have the picture-perfect family. But you need to be aware of the other side of adoption.

You may have been struggling for months, even years, with your inability to have a child. Your heartache is deep and real. At one point, I was told that I might not ever be able to have a child. I remember the cold chill that ran through my heart. I remember the disappointment I felt month after month. I was consumed with my own situation, and because of this, I was not particularly interested in the sorrows of someone else.

Perhaps that is how you feel now. Your heartache and anticipation are all-consuming. But I ask you to take just a moment to try to see the bigger picture. What does it look like from the perspective of a scared, often confused, pregnant teenager?

Recommendations

Have a strong support network for the journey.
Thoroughly educate yourself about the issues.
Take care of yourself in every way and let others help you.
Pray through all of your decisions.

Notes

1. "Major Causes of Infertility," BabyCentre. http://www.babycentre.co.uk/general/6020.html (accessed March 2006).
2. "Causes of Infertility," *Advanced Fertility Center of Chicago.* http://www.advancedfertility.com/infert.htm (accessed March 2006).
3. Jennifer Ehrle Macomber, Erica Zielewsi, Kate Chambers and Rob Geen, "An Analysis of Interest in Adoption and a Review of State Recruitment Strategies," Urban Institute. http://www.urban.org/Publications/411254.html (accessed December 2005).

CHAPTER 2

Adoption Is the Heart of God

Vindicate the weak and fatherless; do justice to the afflicted and destitute.
PSALM 82:3, *NASB*

SARA

As we read the Bible, we can see from passages such as Deuteronomy 24:19 that there are certain people who seem to have a special place in God's heart:

> When you are harvesting in your field and you overlook a sheaf, do not go back to get it. Leave it for the alien, the fatherless and the widow, so that the Lord your God bless you in all the work of your hands.

As we move to the New Testament, we see from passages such as James 1:27-28 that "religion that God our Father accepts as pure and faultless is this: to look after orphans and widows in their distress and to keep oneself from being polluted by the world." God wants us to follow His example. Anyone who has placed his or her trust in Jesus as Lord and Savior has been adopted into the family of God. In other words, we are *all* adopted. Adoption is the heart of God.

Laws governing adoption were introduced into our culture in the mid-nineteenth century. (Unfortunately, there are some states in which the laws seem to be stuck there.) In those days, it was an issue that people didn't talk about openly. It was shameful for a young woman to find herself pregnant and unmarried. Often, to save face, she was sent to live with a distant relation or in a home for unwed mothers. After the birth, the baby would most often be given up for adoption, and the young woman would never speak of it again.

Today, approximately 125,000 children are adopted in the United States every year. It is estimated that for every child available, there are 3 to 4 families trying to adopt that child.[1] Adoption, of course, carries a positive connotation in that it allows a child to live instead of being aborted, enables families to be formed, and restores the dignity of the birthmother. To a young couple struggling with infertility, adoption might be the only way to have a family. However, "adoption" is also a word that has a variety of emotions attached to it, not all of which are positive and good.

If you are a 15-year-old scared and pregnant young girl, the thought of releasing your child to adoption is so frightening that you wouldn't even be able to entertain the idea without incredible sadness and tears. Unfortunately, our society and the media do not help to project a positive image of what adoption is all about. More often than not, all we hear about are the children who have been adopted and who have "gone bad," or about the parents who adopt children and then abuse them. We hear about the birthparents changing their minds and see the two-year-old being ripped from the arms of the only parents he or she has ever known.

However, for every one of those stories, there are hundreds of adoption stories with peaceful and happy endings. Adoption can be a win-win situation for everyone involved. Those for whom adoption has been a positive experience, whether they are the adoptee, adopter or the birthmother, need to speak out and help to create a more positive image and picture of what adoption can be.

Firsthand experience tells me that there are certain elements that will make a regular adoption into a great adoption. For instance, it's a great adoption experience when everyone comes away feeling as though he or she has been touched by the hand of God. Another element that creates a great adoption is when an adoptive couple truly respects the birthparents, especially the birthmother. This respect includes being there when the birthmother needs them to be but also knowing when *not* to be there. One birthmother put it this way: "I knew [the adoptive couple] were there and that I could call them anytime with anything, but I also felt as though they respected my situation and my privacy." Showing this respect helps the birthmother walk the very hard road she must walk after she has chosen the adoptive parents of her unborn child.

Are You Ready to Adopt?

If you have come to the place in which you think and/or know that you are ready to adopt, there are a number of things you need to first consider. The first question that you need to consider is why you want to adopt a child. Now, this would seem to have a simple answer: "Because I want to have children and I am unable to have them the old-fashioned way." However, this is not always enough of an answer.

I once interviewed a couple in their late thirties who were considering adoption. They were successful scientists with a chemical company and had been busy "finding cures for a myriad of illnesses," as they put it. Both of them had received several academic degrees. They had married late and then laid out a clear plan for the rest of their lives. They owned two large houses, one of which was on the water, and two cars. These people were on the fast track to success. Now, they had discovered that they were not able to have children, so they decided to adopt. When I asked the wife how long she intended to stay home with her baby, she assured me that she would stay home a minimum of six weeks, maybe more. At that point, I suggested that they get a Golden Retriever. In their case, a child was an afterthought, something to round out their already perfect life. This should not be the reason to adopt.

The most important decision you will ever make, with the exception of your decision to accept Christ, is to have children, by whatever means. Unlike husbands and wives in today's divorce-ridden world, children are forever. You can't divorce your children, and you can't sell them on eBay. Your children are yours for the duration. Their reason for being is not to make your perfect life even more perfect. Children are a gift from God (a fact about which you may need to be constantly reminded when they become teenagers). Eda Le Shan, a U.S. educator, wrote this in her book *The Conspiracy Against Childhood*:

> Babies are necessary to grown-ups. A new baby is like the beginning of all things—wonder, hope, a dream of possibilities. In a world that is cutting down its trees to build highways, losing its earth to concrete—babies are almost the only remaining link with nature, with the natural world of living things from which we spring.[2]

Another aspect of adoption that you will need to prayerfully and thoughtfully consider is exactly what you want and expect in the adoption experience. Movies seem to either glamorize the adoption process or make it look like a nightmare. It is usually neither—although it can be both. Every adoption is different, because the people involved in each adoption are different. Couples that have adopted more than one child will tell you that each situation has presented very different challenges—and very different benefits. If you want to adopt a child in order to make your Christmas card photo look more like a Norman Rockwell portrait, you need to stop and think. If you are interested in adoption because you truly believe God is calling you to open your heart and home to a child and that you can provide a better life for that child than he or she may currently have, then I would still say to keep thinking.

Adoption is often referred to as "having children the easy way." This is typically said by those people who have either never done it themselves or who have no knowledge of what it takes to do it. I truly believe that if every couple who wanted a child had to go through what adoptive couples do to have a child, there would be only one child in most families. It is by far *not* the easy way. That is why there must be a unified, well-considered agreement between both parents that adoption is the right and best path for them to take. Just as parenting works best when the parents are unified, so does the often long and arduous, even painful, adoption journey.

Staying in God's Plan

Once you have given as much thought, prayer and research to this process as you can stand (and believe me, it can be a never-ending job if you allow it to be), you will need to take the actual steps of beginning the adoption process. As you begin this journey, please keep one thought in mind: If God intends for you to have a child, you will. If He is calling you to adopt and has prepared your heart for this, He has a child just for you. It is not unheard of for a couple, after having accepted as God's will their inability to have children "the old-fashioned way," to discover that now—guess what—they're pregnant. God has a plan for your life, and if children are to be a part of that life, just cooperate with His voice and follow His lead.

Don't run ahead of what you know to be God's plan. You will get lost. If you believe adoption is God's will for you, you need only be obedient to what you believe He is telling you. The outcome of your obedience is His responsibility.

The Bible says that God formed us in our mother's womb and knows the exact number of days we will be here (see Ps. 139:13,16). If you believe this, then you can also believe that there is a child out there whose days are numbered in your care. I recently spoke with a birthmother who said that she knew almost from the beginning of her pregnancy that she would choose adoption. Only once did she feel any sense of loss: when she handed her daughter over to the adoptive mother at the dedication service. It was then that she realized the finality of her decision, but she has never regretted her decision and is completely at peace with what she did. She feels as though she was meant to carry this child for this exact couple, and she also feels that this exact couple was God's choice as adoptive parents for her daughter.

RUTH

When my teenage daughter, Windsor, sat beside me on my bed that sunny November day and told me she was pregnant, my first thoughts were to embrace her, protect her and nurture her. I then began to think ahead, and it wasn't hard for me to recognize that she was not ready to be a mother. And I knew that the young man was not going to shoulder his responsibility as a father. To me, that left only two options: I would enable Windsor to rear the child, taking on many of her responsibilities, or she would decide to release her baby for adoption.

It was Windsor's decision to make. It is the birthmother's right to make that choice: to parent or to release—or, in our society, to abort. Windsor chose life. Now, we had to decide the future course of our lives and the precious new life growing within her.

The only decision that was mine to make was whether or not I would help Windsor rear this child. How does one make such a decision? This was my grandchild and, emotionally, I wanted that child. The happiest times in my life had been when I gave birth and had a little one in the house. I could envision the joy a baby would bring. But was this the best idea?

I had to clear my head, step back, and try to be objective as I evaluated what was best for the baby, for me, and, in the long run, for Windsor. I counseled with the man who was then my pastor, and he advised me to go before the Lord and ask Him to direct me. I laid it all out before the Lord and asked Him to show me what was best.

Windsor desperately wanted me to say that she could keep the baby and help her raise it. For her, it was simple—and it was emotional. I appeared to be standing between her and her baby. For me, it was far more complex. I knew that there were other things to consider: Windsor's young age and lack of experience; her circle of friends; her compliance, or lack thereof, with house rules . . . I knew that our relationship was far too volatile to allow for any successful measure of co-parenting.

I had to ask and answer the questions: Would Windsor get a job? Stay in school? Would she want to date? How much childcare was I willing to do? To what extent would I be responsible? What about medical bills? Would Windsor obey my rules?

At the time, I was working full-time for Samaritan's Purse. I was going to school, trying to finish my college degree. And I had a new marriage. My husband and I discussed how to handle this. He loved Windsor like a daughter. He loved me, but there was no way he was willing to raise a baby at that stage in his life. I didn't think that we could take on Windsor's baby under all of these circumstances.

But beyond the factors of being newly married, working full-time and going to college, the most important factor was simply this: Had God called me to rear this baby? I truly wrestled with my decision. I tried to visualize all scenarios. My emotions pulled me in all directions. Of course I wanted that baby! Of course I wanted to cuddle it and watch it grow up. Above all, I am a nurturer.

One day as I sat with my Bible, asking God to show me what to do, I became deeply impressed that I was *not* to take on the consequences of Windsor's behavior or the responsibility for her child.

My decision became conviction. I never wavered, but my heart did break.

Recommendations

Pray for guidance.
Research your options.
Talk to others who have adopted.
Listen to His voice.

Notes

1. U.S. Census data, 2000. http://www.census.gov/ (accessed March 2006).
2. Eda Le Shan, *The Conspiracy Against Childhood* (New York: Atheneum, 1967), n.p.

CHAPTER 3

The Type of Adoption That Is Best for You

Man looks at the outward appearance, but the LORD looks at the heart.
1 SAMUEL 16:7

SARA

The thought of adopting a child can be a frightening prospect for women. Perhaps this is why of all the women who have ever considered adoption (as many as 10 million), only 2 percent have ever actually begun the process.[1] This is one of the reasons why we decided to write this book—to make this scary journey a little less frightening and hopefully to make the process a little easier.

Don't be lulled into a false sense that adoption can or should be a trouble-free way to create a family. It is not. Some adoptions go very smoothly, while others appear to be train wrecks waiting to happen. You don't know which one yours will be, but the best philosophy is to prepare for the worst and pray for the best. For all the years that I have been working with young women and for all the couples I have seen adopt, there is one thing I can say without hesitation: There is a God and He is in control. If you are meant to adopt, there is only one thing you can do to derail the process, and that is to not listen to the voice of God as He speaks to you.

There are two basic types of adoption: international adoption and domestic adoption (which includes foster-care adoption). In an international adoption, someone who holds American citizenship adopts a child from a country outside of the United States. In a domestic adoption, the child is an American citizen who is being adopted from one of the 50 states in the United States.

Both international and domestic adoptions are viable options to consider, but each requires a different mind-set at the outset of the process. For instance, many people want to adopt a child who will look just like them. Is this possible? Yes, it is. In fact, I know a family whose first child looks *exactly* like his adoptive father. But those who adopt internationally do not have this expectation. It is highly unlikely that their child will look like them.

International Adoption

There are many agencies that specialize in international adoptions for a particular country. It is important to be comfortable with the agency and to work with one that has experience for the country in which you are interested. International adoptions can cost more than $20,000 and will often involve you spending weeks away from home in a foreign country, waiting for your child.

If either time or money is an issue for you, international adoption might not be for you. These adoptions can be both time-consuming and money-consuming, and they do not provide the adoptive parents with much, if any, medical information about the biological parents of the child. Granted, you will not have to endure the difficult waiting period from the time of birth until the birthparents' rights have been terminated, which is a big feature in domestic adoptions.

Many couples are willing to trade off having background information about their child's parents for the peace of mind of not having to endure the emotional roller coaster of waiting for the parents' rights to be terminated. But you do have to consider that many of the children in international adoptions may be a little older, and many may suffer from attachment disorder due to the lack of bonding with an adult. Of course, such problems can be overcome with time, love and specialized counseling, when necessary. Many or most of the children in international adoptions are placed in orphanages before they are adopted. In some cases, they have become part of the foster-care system of their countries.

Thirty-five percent of all babies adopted internationality are from either Korea (24 percent) or China (11 percent).[2] We have all heard stories of the thousands of little girls in China that await a forever family somewhere in this world. In China, the government has established a one child per family policy, and because parents in that nation typically prefer to have boys, more baby girls than boys are placed in orphanages to allow the family to try to have a baby boy. I suspect that at some point, the Chinese government will realize that all of these baby boys are going to need baby girls to keep the country going. However, with a population of more than 1.7 billion, that does not appear to be an immediate problem. What this means for international adoptions from China is that there are more girls than boys waiting for adoption.

When you adopt from another country, one of the issues that you will need to consider is how you are going to preserve that child's sense of nationality and heritage. This applies not only to international adoptions but also to domestic biracial adoptions. Many white couples I meet live in a "white bread" neighborhood and feel that a child of a different race would have a difficult time fitting in to that environment. If you feel that such an adoption will not work, then it won't work. If you are white and you want to adopt a child from a black, Indian or other ethnic background, it is important to understand that child's original heritage and culture. Many people feel uncomfortable adopting internationally for that reason: They worry how they will teach that child about who he or she is.

I believe that we are living in a world today where such "white bread" neighborhoods are becoming fewer. As citizens of this world, we are going to need to learn to live in harmony with people from all nationalities and to appreciate the cultural roots of others.

Domestic Adoption

Domestic adoption can be divided into three types: public adoption, private adoption, and agency adoption.

Public Adoption

Public adoption occurs when children from the child welfare system are placed in permanent homes. This can be done through a state-run agency or private agency with a state contract. This type of adoption, also referred to as "foster-care adoption," is not for the faint of heart. You might get an infant or young child and have him or her with you for years, only to have the parents get that child back at a later time. Needless to say, this can be heartbreaking.

It has been said that if a couple from every evangelical church in this country adopted just one child currently in foster care, there would be no more children in the foster-care system. Of the 500,000 children in the system, approximately 130,000 to 150,000 are considered available for adoption.[3] The majority of these children are older, and many have emotional or physical problems. These children are usually in the foster-care system because of abuse, abandonment or neglect.

These are the children that you really need to pray about and be sure that you have been called to adopt. Since these children have already had a lifetime of hurt and rejection, they may be difficult to raise. This type of adoption is about providing a child with a loving, stable home and trusting the Lord for the details.

Public adoptions are free (or at least inexpensive), but there is the risk of a custody conflict after placement. I have a friend who began fostering a baby boy when he was six weeks old. Every time his mother was about to lose custody of him, which meant my friend would be able to adopt him, the birthmother would do whatever she could to keep the process from being resolved. This course of action continued for 14 years until the adoption could be finalized. This is an extreme case, but it illustrates my point.

The adoption process for these children will vary from state to state. If public adoption is something that the Lord might be calling you to do, contact the Child and Youth Services in your county.

Private Adoption

In a private adoption, an attorney or facilitator arranges the adoption without the involvement of an adoption agency. In some states, adoption agencies are required by law to be involved in the process, so if you are considering this type of adoption, you must consult the laws of your state and the state where the birthmother lives. In some states, private facilitators are not permitted, so again, it is very important to know the laws of your particular state. Private domestic adoptions are, as a rule, less expensive than international or agency-facilitated adoptions.

An open adoption occurs when the adoptive parents have the opportunity to meet with the birthmother and birthfather and establish some sort of relationship with them. This provides the adoptive parents with the opportunity to get to know the woman who has decided to release her child into the adoptive parent's family. This can aid in the healing process for the birthparents and their circle of support.

When an open adoption is handled privately rather than through an agency, you can keep the cost of adoption to a reasonable level. A private adoption, achieved without the services of an agency, should cost less than $10,000. Adoption costs can and should be provided in advance. (In some states, the adoptive parents are permitted to financially help the birthmother, which will add to the cost.) As I mentioned, state laws vary, so it is important to have an adoption attorney advise you as to the laws that apply to your specific case. (We will discuss open adoption in greater detail in chapter 5.)

Agency Adoption
An agency adoption is just that—an adoption in which a licensed adoption agency is used either by the birthmother to help her find a family, by the adoptive family to help them find a birthmother, or by both. This type of adoption does tend to be somewhat more expensive, but the cost is still within the reach of most people. As you prepare your budget for this process, it is important that you have a pretty good idea of which type of adoption you want to pursue.

Costs of Adoption

If you sat down and honestly listed the cost of having a child from diapers to college, you would realize that almost no one could afford children, regardless of whether they are biological or adopted. This is a persistent misconception about adoption—that it is only for the wealthy and that the average person cannot afford to adopt a child. It is true that the majority of adoptions cost more than $10,000, but I worked with a family that adopted three healthy infants, and all three adoptions combined were under $25,000—so it can be done. This is why it is important to prepare a realistic budget and question any fees or expenses, whether they come through an agency, from an attorney, or by way of your state.

In most situations, the birthmother will be covered by her own insurance or will be insured by her parents. In cases where the birthmother has no insurance, she will be eligible for Medicaid, and she and the baby will be covered until the placement of the baby. Some insurance companies will only pay for 80 percent of the related expenses, in which case the adoptive family will usually be asked to cover those additional costs. There are foundations and other organizations that can provide financial resources for those who wish to adopt.

I was once involved in an adoption in which the baby had a perforated colon at birth and had to be flown to a big city hospital for care. He was in the NICU for nearly three weeks, and the bill for his care was rapidly mounting. The adoptive parents never wavered in their commitment to this baby. When the treatment was nearing completion, they were told the bill would be in the $80,000 range. As they prepared to refinance their home, I contacted a friend who had connections at the hospital, and they were able to have the baby put on Medicaid retroactively. The bill was paid. This is the way that God can answer your prayers. If there is a child out there who is meant to be part of your family, there is nothing too hard for the Lord to do in creating this forever family.

RUTH

Windsor was adamant—she was going to keep her baby. She tried to negotiate with me, with her father, with the baby's father, with her counselor. She begged, she pleaded, she threatened.

Slowly, her options ran out. As hard as it was, she had to face reality. She was not going to be able to rear this baby on her own. She couldn't cajole anyone to do it for her. The friends that had promised to stand by her drifted away.

This was a difficult time for everyone. She blamed me, especially, and she vented her anger often. More and more, I believed my decision was the right one.

I was invited to Sara's house in Philadelphia to be part of a surprise birthday luncheon for two of our mutual friends. The daughter of another friend had flown in to surprise her mother. It was a happy time. This group of ladies gets together several times a year, gathering for lunch and an afternoon of conversation, laughter, prayer and, sometimes, tears. We talk about current issues, politics, books, family and concerns of our hearts. These are dear friendships that have spanned years.

Over lunch, I confided to these friends that Windsor was pregnant. The ladies were supportive and loving. The surprise guest who had flown in, Vickie, looked at me thoughtfully and told me that this child was going to be very special. I didn't pay much attention to her comment—but I did remember it.

Although I had known Sara for a number of years, I did not know (or I had forgotten) the fact that she is a clinical psychologist who specializes in helping people who are dealing with unplanned pregnancies. She had often taken young pregnant women into her home to live with her family during their pregnancy. Once she reminded me of that, I peppered her with questions. Here was a one-stop source of answers to all the questions I had—and some I didn't have! This was a wonderful, unexpected, hopeful turn of events for me.

During our time together, Vickie had a side conversation with Sara and told her about a couple in her Bible study who were trying to adopt a child. Sara suggested to Vickie that she tell the couple to send their profile so that Sara could see what she could do to help them.

The week after the luncheon, the phone rang. Sara was on the other end. She said that she had talked to her husband and their two teenaged boys, and she wondered if I would consider letting Windsor live with them for the remainder of her pregnancy. What a gift!

I removed Windsor from the home for unwed mothers where she had been living and drove her to Sara's house. She became part of their family. Sara walked her though the myriad of pregnancy issues and major decisions and at the same time homeschooled her so that Windsor would be able to keep up with her class at school.

While at Sara's house, Windsor became acquainted with other young women who had faced or were facing the same situation. This was a level of support that I was unable to offer her at home. I will always be grateful for Sara—she made an eternal difference in our lives.

When Windsor was about six months into her pregnancy, Sara happened to be counseling a young woman whose due date was about a month earlier than Windsor's. This young woman had decided to release her baby for adoption and was in the process of choosing a forever family for her child. She was evaluating profiles of couples that Sara had in a file.

One afternoon after the young woman left Sara's house, Windsor asked Sara if she could see the file of profiles of prospective parents. She leafed through the file quietly, thoughtfully. After some time, she pulled out a profile and told Sara, "If I were going to release my baby, this is the couple I would choose."

Recommendations

Prepare a budget.

Decide which type of adoption best suits you.

Prepare a realistic timeline to complete the process.

Be patient and trust God's plan.

Notes
1. Mary Jo Sylwester, "U.S. Census Bureau Data 2000 Analysis," *USA Today*, August 25, 2003.
2. Ibid.
3. Ibid.

CHAPTER 4

The Journey Begins

Every prudent man acts out of knowledge.
PROVERBS 13:16

SARA

When I was in the midst of answering countless phone calls the night my interview was on *Delilah,* I realized that there were a lot of very compassionate people out there who, if asked, would gladly welcome a child into their homes. It didn't seem to be an issue of, "I want to have a child to complete me" as much as, "Here are some children that need a forever home, and I can provide one of those." However, I also realized that these people had no clue whatsoever about the eligibility requirements for adoption.

Quite naturally, adoption is uncharted territory for most people. Making a good decision is impossible without first gathering as much information as you can. The problem with this is that you could spend the next two years of your life gathering information—and some of it would change while you were still gathering it. This is why you need to be as focused as possible before you actually begin the process.

As you recognize that you are willing to open your hearts and home to a child, the process of focusing begins with you and your spouse setting down the parameters with which both of you feel comfortable. Of course, you will need to develop a budget, but there are other considerations as well: How old should the child be? Do you want a baby only, or are you willing to adopt an older child? Do you want a boy or a girl—or does it matter? Must the child be of the same race as you and your spouse? Can you handle a child who has some disabilities? Do you care whether or not the mother used drugs, alcohol or cigarettes?

Each variable you add to or subtract from this picture will possibly affect how long you will wait for a child. For example, if you want a blond-haired, blue-eyed, Caucasian baby boy whose mother was a virgin until she conceived him, you may have a longer wait than if you are willing to adopt a child of either sex, any race, any age and whose mother was not the Virgin Mary.

Both you and your spouse must agree to these parameters. You don't want to find yourself in a situation in which either of you disagree about what you have decided about an issue or one in which either of you feels talked into something that is uncomfortable for you. This is a lifetime commitment, so every particular must be made by mutual agreement. It will also be very important for you and your spouse to pray together during this process. Once you have established these parameters, you need to begin what is referred to as a "home study" and also begin to prepare a profile.

Your Home Study

There are four main purposes for doing a home study: (1) to educate you on the adoption process; (2) to prepare you for adoption; (3) to gather information about you and your spouse that will help to match you with a child whose needs you and your spouse can meet; and (4) to evaluate your fitness as the adoptive family. The home study makes it possible to present a document to the court that shows you are financially, emotionally and mentally stable, as well as physically healthy. It also shows that you would (in the opinion of friends who will write letters of reference and the social worker who will visit your home) make wonderful parents and would provide a secure, happy home for a child.

Just to put this step in perspective: I once had a client who was with the Secret Service and had been charged with guarding the president of the United States. He said that the home study for adoption was more thorough and taxing than his Secret Service clearance had been. Now, if that doesn't have you rethinking your desire to adopt—let's move on!

A home study is a document required by law for domestic adoptions in all 50 states and also for all international adoptions.

Again, since the laws for adoption vary by state, you should first check with either a licensed adoption agency or an agency that does home studies. Both of these can be found in the yellow pages of your phone book. In some states, a licensed social worker can do the home study as long as he or she is on the approved court list. In some states, an agency is required to not only do the study but also to be actively involved in the process.

This home study step will take anywhere from three to six months to complete. You cannot have a child placed in your home without it, so if you are serious about adoption, you must undergo this process. The cost of having a home study done can vary, but you will probably be safe to budget $1,000 to $3,000 for it. If you have an adoption agency do the home study for you and work with and through them to find a birthmother, the cost might be somewhat less than if you have them only do the home study. Be sure you understand what the agency expects of you and that you understand what they are willing to provide. Some agencies will require you to sign an agreement that you will work only with them; others won't care. Read the fine print before you sign anything with anyone.

The home study is a paper-intensive task that will require time, patience and a sense of humor—three qualities that you will also need in abundance to raise a child. The areas that will be covered in your home study may vary by state (or even by county), but it will most likely include the following:

- **Parent training classes:** These help you to understand a child's needs and help you decide what type of child you can parent best.
- **Interviews:** These may be individual or joint interviews or both. Interviews will help the social worker better understand your family and assist you with an appropriate placement.

- **Home visit:** This is to make sure your home meets your state licensing requirements. Oftentimes, the home visit and the interview can be done at the same time.
- **Health statements:** You will be required to have a complete physical to show that you will have a normal life expectancy and that you are physically and mentally able to care for a child.
- **Income statements:** The requirements here may vary from simple pay stubs to complete income tax forms. The purpose of an income statement is to prove that you are financially stable and that you handle your finances responsibly.
- **Background check:** A criminal and child abuse background check must be done for obvious reasons. In some states, local, state and federal clearances are required. The social worker doing your home study will know what is required.
- **Autobiography:** You will have to write an autobiography, an abbreviated story of your life. Again this is to help whoever is helping you to make a good match.
- **References:** The person or agency will ask you to supply names and addresses of people you know in various aspects of your life to provide them with a range of references. These will give the social worker a well-rounded picture of your family.

The home study will include all aspects of who you are, including your family background, your education, your employment and your religion. Once the social worker has collected all the material, he or she will write the home-study report, and you will either be approved or not. Most families are approved. If there are problems, you will most likely know before the study is complete.

Your home study will be valid for at least a year. Again, state laws differ, so it is important for you to investigate the specific laws in your own state. If your home study should expire before a child has been placed in your home, you will need to do an update. The person or agency that did your original home study can easily and quickly do the update for you. The update will address any significant changes to your situation, such as a job change, a move and the like.

Your Profile

A profile is a one- to two-page document that contains you and your spouse's photograph (and any children that you already have) and a very brief biographical sketch of you and your spouse. The purpose of this profile is to give the birthmother some idea about who you are and to generate enough interest in you that she will want to talk to you directly. I can't stress enough the importance of this document—the photograph in particular.

I have seen young women pick up a profile and never read it, because they didn't like the "look" of the couple. One young girl didn't like the type of dog in the picture and rejected the couple for that reason alone. Does this seem unfair and unreasonable? Yes! But unfortunately, that's how it is, and the birthmother is the one who makes the decision. Most birthmothers want more than anything to keep their babies, so they are going to look for reasons to reject you in order to be forced to parent their children themselves because there are no "acceptable" families out there.

RUTH

When a birthmother is in the process of deciding to release her baby into the arms of a stranger, she has many questions about the people she will choose to rear her child. As a potential adoptive parent, some of her questions may seem irrelevant and intrusive to you, but for the birthmother they are vital.

Think about it. I am sure that you want to know as much about the birthmother and her family as you can find out. There are the obvious concerns, such as health and mental stability. But there may also be some unique things that you may want to know: Does she have a musical gift? Does she prefer dogs or cats?

She wants to know some of these same things about you.

Sara has mentioned the importance of writing out a profile with a photo attached and going through the process of a home study. For weeks and months, the profile you create will provide the only facts that the birthmother knows about you. The importance of this profile cannot be overstated—it either gets you in the door or it doesn't. Your life will change on the basis of that paperwork. It seems cruel that so much hinges on so little.

As Sara has stated, you cannot take God out of the equation. It is purely a God-thing when a young woman looks at a single page of words and decides that *you* are the couple she will choose to raise her child. God can make inconsequential details jump off of a page and touch a young woman's heart. I don't understand how it works; I just know that it does.

From reading through profiles and information, Windsor knew which couple appealed to her. The profile gave her a first impression of who they were—and first impressions can make or break this kind of situation. From the photo, she saw that the lady was blonde (as she is) and that the man was handsome. The couple looked happy, nice and intelligent. The photo was very important!

In addition, although Windsor was still far from decided about the release of her baby, the profile made her curious to know more. As Windsor read the information in the brief profile, she liked the couple even more than she had from her first impression of the photo. She wanted to meet them.

When Windsor showed me the profile of the couple she was considering, I agreed with her choice. It was only one page with a photo taking up about a fourth of the page, so the information had been boiled down to the essentials they wanted a birthmother to know. I liked what they chose to say about themselves and how it seemed to dovetail with who Windsor was. I liked their looks. Their information was not heavy—they kept it light and friendly but to the point. They mentioned briefly that they had been trying to have a child for 10 years, but to no avail. They mentioned their professions and hobbies. They wrote that they were willing to make the changes necessary to have a child in their home.

We did not see the home-study paperwork, as it is not usually something the birthmother sees. But we knew that a thorough study had been done, and we felt secure in that knowledge. Because a social worker is trained to do a home study, he or she would have asked questions that we would never have thought to ask. We knew that the home study would have been thorough and deliberate and that it would have disclosed anything that could become troublesome down the road.

I am sure that for the prospective parents in Windsor's situation, the many questions and all the probing into their private life must have seemed like trespassing. At times it must have been maddening to them, but we knew that the home study was a wonderful tool to make sure the family and birthmother fit together and were making a good decision for the baby. When you submit to such intrusion, you are demonstrating your seriousness about wanting to provide the best possible home for your future child. That seriousness and commitment speak volumes to a birthmother and her family.

Knowing that a complete and thorough home study had been done made us feel secure that we were not handing the baby to complete strangers. A lot was known about them. Based on that assurance, Windsor could make an informed decision.

Recommendations

Keep the paperwork moving.

Tell everyone you know that you want to adopt.

Stay positive, but realistic.

Pray with and for your spouse.

CHAPTER 5

Open Adoption: To Know or Not to Know

I also have lent him to the LORD; as long as he lives
he shall be lent to the LORD.
1 SAMUEL 1:28, *NKJV*

SARA

As a prospective adoptive parent, merely hearing the term "open adoption" can make you feel anxious. Before you venture into this area, you need to understand that there are degrees of openness involved in the process of open adoption. You will need to decide whether or not you will be comfortable with a particular degree of openness for the near and, possibly, distant future.

Many adoption professionals feel that openness among those involved in the adoption—birthparents, adoptive parents and child—is healthier for everyone in both the long-term and the short-term. Research shows that families who have participated in open adoption list several benefits:

- For the adoptive parents, there is greater freedom from the "sleeping with one eye open" syndrome (worrying about the birthparents returning to claim their child).
- Children are generally clear about who their parents are. With an open adoption, the adoptive parents can share with their child any information they may want to about that child's biological parents.
- When the birthparents take an active role in the selection of the family in which the child will grow up, they feel more confident about their decision.
- Generally, open adoptions, although they may seem somewhat riskier to the adopting parents, allow the birthparents to deal better with their grief and give them a sense of control when everything else seems out of control.
- Open adoptions give the birthparents peace of mind because they know where and with whom their child will be placed.

In one adoption I facilitated, prior to the birth of the child, the adoptive parents held a family picnic for the birthmother in which she had the opportunity to meet the aunts, uncles, cousins and grandparents of the family in which her daughter would be raised. For the birthmother, it was painful, but equally reassuring, to see the family in which her daughter would grow up. She also had the opportunity to see her daughter when she was 18 months old, something not too many birthmothers get to do. This was a *very* open adoption.

How Open Is Open Adoption?

In open adoption, there is a continuum from semi-open to very open. It is critical that you decide what you will be comfortable with over the long haul and also what the birthmother will expect from you. Obviously, adoptive couples are going to feel comfortable with varying levels of openness. But I firmly believe there is a direct correlation between the openness of the adoptive couple and their trust that the Lord has orchestrated this process.

At the least, most birthmothers want letters and pictures on a regular basis, and most adoptive parents agree to this. These pictures and letters are extremely important to the birthmother, and everyone needs to have a clear understanding of everyone else's expectations from the beginning. I have known situations in which the adoptive parents were still sending pictures and letters after 10 years and other cases in which the adoptive parents and birthmother drifted apart.

While receiving these letters and pictures from the adoptive couple is very important, it will be difficult for the birthmother to see what someone else is able to provide for her child that she was not able to provide. However, great reassurance also comes in seeing firsthand the wonderful life that the birthmother has chosen for her child.

I once introduced a birthmother who was to give her testimony at a Crisis Pregnancy Center fund-raising dinner. She came up to speak and tell why she had chosen life over abortion and why she was choosing adoption over parenting. When she was finished, she said, "And now, I would like you to meet the mother of my baby." Up to the podium came the woman that she and the birthfather had chosen to become the parent of their child. There was not a dry eye in the house, including mine.

Of course, it isn't always going to seem that perfect. No matter how sure everyone is that adoption is absolutely the very best choice for everyone involved, it still involves loss, and it still brings pain. It is a death of sorts. Grief is the natural by-product of any death.

When you ask a birthmother if she wants to have an open adoption, her immediate answer is almost always yes. However, what she imagines this process will be like is probably going to look much different from what you might be thinking. The truth is that in the fantasy world of the young pregnant girl, she wants you to have and raise her child—but to also allow her to be able to see, talk to, write to, and eventually get to know her child as if she had never been out of the picture. Quite naturally, this would make any adoptive couple feel uncomfortable.

In reality, in most open adoptions, the birthparents take an active role in choosing the adoptive parents of their child. They review profiles, meet couples and eventually make a choice. Once their child is placed, they can expect to exchange letters and photos—and that's all. This is what the vast majority of open adoptions look like.

Further up the scale of openness, the arrangement can include occasional visits when the child is still young. Even further up the scale of openness are those adoptions in which the birthmother is an active presence in her child's life. I should say that I do not think that this is the best situation for those involved because it tends to lead to the bond between birthmother and her child never being broken and the bond between the adoptive parents and the child never being cemented.

The following is a letter from a birthmother to the couple who adopted her daughter. You can see from reading it that this was a win-win adoption, which is what everyone wants. This letter was sent to the adoptive parents after the birthmother had received some birthday pictures and a letter from them.

Hello all,

Thank you so much! She is absolutely beautiful! (Of course, I would think so, hee hee.)

And I think the birthday cake is great. Whose idea was that? I would love to see some of the whole family at some point. How are Dylan and Gracie doing? I know you guys send yearly letters and will answer all of these questions, so I'll just wait, but I wanted to say thanks again and that my parents and I loved the pictures. You guys rock!

Thanks so much for the blessing you've given me and my family. I can't thank you all enough. You are the most wonderful couple in the whole world. I have such peace every day knowing that my sticky situation ended so wonderfully well. People always ask if it's hard for me to look at pictures, and I can't explain enough how it feels as though I'm looking at someone else's child. I feel as if I were a surrogate mother for you two and that she was always meant to be there with your family. It just fits. I couldn't be happier.

Much love,

Joy

The young girl who wrote this letter was the daughter of a pastor. She graduated from a Christian school, and through this situation, she was able to see God's hand at work in her life as well as in the life of her daughter. God is a God of second chances, and both this young woman and her daughter have been given a wonderful second chance. This is an unusual situation, but certainly not unheard of in the adoption world.

Have Clear Expectations

How well individuals involved in the adoption process handle the situation depends a great deal on how well they have been counseled and prepared for the journey. I'll say it again: It is extremely important that the parties involved—the adoptive parents and the birthparents—are clear about what they want as well as what they expect.

This preparation is the responsibility of whoever is working with the birthparents, whether it is the adoption agency, the facilitator or an attorney. It is critical that the birthparents receive counseling by a professional as often as possible during the pregnancy. While there is nothing that can ever prepare a young woman for the feelings she will experience when she releases her child into the arms of another woman, there are some things that a professional can at least try to prepare her for.

As an adoptive couple, you need to make it clear to the agency or the attorney the parameters with which you are comfortable. If you want a boy, that is fine. If you want a Caucasian boy, that also is fine. If you are not comfortable with a birthmother who has used or is using drugs, let them know. There are birthmothers who receive no prenatal care and who drink, smoke and use drugs and yet, through God's grace, give birth to healthy babies. However, most potential parents are not willing to take that kind of risk if they don't have to.

As adoptive parents, you, most of all, need to be comfortable with your decision. This is a lifetime commitment, and one that is far too important to make lightly.

RUTH

As I reviewed the profile of the couple and examined their photo, I liked Windsor's choice. They seemed very suitable, and I began to pray for them. From what they had written in their profile, I knew they longed for a baby.

Windsor picked this couple out from all the others because, as she states, "he was a lawyer and I wanted to be a lawyer. She was a special-education teacher and I have learning difficulties. They were young, and he looked like he would be a wonderful dad. They presented themselves in such a way that they really stood out."

But there was only one way that Windsor was going to release her child for adoption—it had to be an open adoption. She would not entertain any idea that she would just hand her child over never to hear from or see the child again. That was not going to happen. She was adamant. I agreed with her. We wanted the reassurance that her child was going to be provided for, nurtured, trained and instructed in the way God designed.

Windsor laid out her desires of what she wanted in an open adoption: letters, pictures, videos. . . . Some of the things she wanted had to be negotiated through Sara.

Most adoptive couples are willing to meet the birthmother half way or beyond. But some requests are unrealistic and would accomplish nothing and create turmoil. You must decide what is best for the child and the stability of the home to which he or she is going.

After Windsor chose the couple, she wanted to meet them face to face. I did too. Since Windsor was living with Sara near Philadelphia, my oldest daughter, Noelle, and I drove up from

Virginia to meet with them. The couple flew in from out of town.

Emotions were close to the surface. This was going to be a life-altering meeting for all of us. How do you behave when you meet the couple that will raise your own flesh and blood? What do you say to the ones who will claim your first grandchild as their own child?

It begins with "Hello."

We sat out on Sara's deck. It was a beautiful spring day—warm sun, cool breezes. We sat across from each other. The woman was blonde and blue-eyed, like Windsor. The man was tall, dark and very intelligent.

We were nervous. Sara did her best to make us comfortable. It was an atmosphere of openness, bridled anticipation and apprehension. Who were these people? They were strangers, and yet we were inviting them into our lives in a radical, life-changing way.

Sara helped facilitate conversation until it began to flow more easily. I could only imagine how difficult this must have been for the couple! Their hearts were right out there—fragile, vulnerable and hopeful . . . oh, so hopeful. Our hearts were right out there—fragile, vulnerable and very anxious.

Soon, though, we were chatting, laughing, enjoying each other like friends. We were feeling more comfortable as Windsor began to ask the questions she needed answered: Would the woman stay home with the baby? Would they allow an open adoption? If so, how open? What were the conditions? Did she want to be in the delivery room?

The couple was very forthcoming and eager to answer any and every question Windsor had. They asked their own questions of her. I had a question that I was hesitant to ask, but one that I knew needed to be addressed. Windsor and I, too, needed to be forthright. It could change everything.

Windsor, Noelle, Sara and I gathered for a minute in Sara's kitchen to talk about this issue. This young couple had no idea of the heritage of Windsor's baby. They needed to be aware that this unborn child was the great-granddaughter of Billy and Ruth Graham. If they made that known to their family and friends, would the child ever be their own, or would people always see Billy Graham in her? Would this make a difference for them?

We went back outside on the deck and explained what the circumstances were and who we were. We asked if this made a difference to them.

Without hesitation, the couple said that it did not. But I did not get the impression that their answer was without some measure of thought. And as far as I know, they have never told anyone this fact; she is completely their child. She even has her "mother's" blue eyes and her "father's" dark hair. She does not really look like Windsor, nor does she look like a Graham. God attends to the details! As the psalmist says in Psalm 103:19, "His sovereignty rules over all" (*NASB*).

I came away believing them to be the right couple. We all did. But Windsor still vacillated about the decision to release her baby. Sara said that was normal.

Recommendations

Talk to people who have adopted children.
Understand what the birthmother wants in a relationship.
Be aware of what your comfort level is regarding openness.
Don't agree to anything the birthmother wants just
to be able to adopt her child.

CHAPTER 6

Legal and Financial Aspects of Adoption

*But when the proper time came God sent his son, born of a human
mother and born under the jurisdiction of the Law, that he might
redeem those who were under the authority of the Law and lead
us into becoming, by adoption, true sons of God.*

GALATIANS 4:4-5, *PHILLIPS*

SARA

Adoption, the process of opening your heart and home to a child, saves another person. It parallels what God has done for each of us by adopting us into His family. However, you cannot escape the fact that adoption involves legal issues. Therefore, it is critical to find an attorney who specializes in adoption law. Just as you would not go to a tax attorney for a divorce, you should not go to any kind of attorney except for one who specializes in adoption law. Only an attorney who specializes in adoptions will know the particular laws for your state and any obscure laws that may apply to your situation.

The American Academy of Adoption Attorneys is a national association of attorneys who practice (or have otherwise distinguished themselves) in the area of adoption law.[1] Not all adoption attorneys belong to this organization, but it is a good place to start to get the help and advice you need. If you are working through an agency, that agency should provide the legal work as a part of their fee. But again, always make sure you read the fine print of any contract you sign.

One young woman I worked with who was considering adoption was asked in a conversation with an adoption attorney whether she had any American Indian blood in her. She said yes, her mother was Cherokee. It turned out that in her state, by law, the Cherokee Nation had to be contacted before an adoption was granted. They had the first right of refusal as to whether or not they would allow a child to be adopted outside of the tribe. At this point, the birthmother became concerned with the uncertainty of what that could mean, so she decided that rather than having her child grow up on a reservation, she would parent the child herself. Before this, she had never paid any attention to her Native American roots, but now she felt that it would be in her child's best interest not to allow an adoption after all.

An attorney who does not specialize in adoption may not have known this fact, and it could have come back to haunt a non-Cherokee adoptive family.

Adoption provides plenty of legal complications. Because legal matters are best addressed by a professional in the field of law, we've asked Debra Fox, Esq., to contribute the following information on this subject.

Debra Fox, Esq.

Because the laws of adoption vary from state to state, no uniform adoption law applies to the entire nation, although common threads link the laws of every state. What follows is an explanation of basic adoption laws, without details about any particular state's law. This is meant to be an introduction to people involved in the process of adoption. For guidance as to the laws of a particular state, please contact an experienced adoption attorney in that state.

Agency Adoption vs. Private Adoption

In addition to public (or "foster care") adoptions discussed in chapter 3, the two types of adoptions available in most states are agency adoptions and private (or independent) adoptions.

In an agency adoption, the birthmother contacts a licensed adoption agency to assist her in finding a family to place her baby for adoption. The advantage of agency adoption is that adoption agencies are licensed by the state and are therefore monitored on an annual basis for compliance with appropriate laws. Most states prohibit licensed adoption agencies from hiring employees who have been convicted of a crime or accused of child abuse. To help birthmothers to thoroughly consider all options besides adoption, such as foster care, parenting or having a family member parent the child, agencies are allowed to provide counseling services to birthparents and adoptive families.

In a private or independent adoption, no agency is involved. Instead, a private adoption attorney handles the case. One disadvantage of private adoption is that in some states, the birthmother may not be able to get counseling. Experience has taught me that one of the single most important parts of a successful adoption is the counseling of the birthmother. Although you can never fully prepare her for what lies ahead, counseling eliminates many of the surprises. If the birthmother's state does not allow adoptive families to reimburse her for counseling expenses (and, because it is a private adoption, no agency will be providing that service), the birthmother may not be able to afford counseling and may not receive it. Even so, for personal reasons some birthparents prefer working with an attorney.

In a private adoption, it is always important to know whom the attorney represents. In most states, due to the inherent conflict of interest, it is illegal for the same attorney to represent both the birthparents and the adoptive family. Usually, the adoptive family hires an attorney and the birthparents have a separate attorney. In certain states, it is legal for the adoptive parents to reimburse the birthparents for legal expenses. However, in states that allow birthparents to forego legal representation, some birthparents choose not to hire their own attorney at all.

The Role of Facilitators

Facilitators operate apart from licensed adoption agencies and attorneys. Adoptive parents hire facilitators, whose services are often advertised in the yellow pages of the phone book, to locate a birthmother who will place her child for adoption with them. However, in most states, facilitators are not allowed do more than match a birthmother with an adoptive family. If they do, they will appear to be operating as an adoption agency without a license. Because facilitators are not licensed, there is no supervision or quality control by the state.

Legal Consent to Adopt

Whether birthparents decide to work with an agency or a private attorney, legal documents will need to be signed. Most (if not all) states require a birthmother to wait until after she delivers her baby to sign a consent to surrender her baby for adoption. This is a protection for the birthmother. The thinking is that after a woman delivers a baby, she goes through emotional and physical changes that could interfere with her ability to make a good, clear, life decision. Waiting periods vary from 24 hours to 10 days. Some states have no waiting period after the baby is born and allow the birthmother to sign a consent immediately.

Consent-signing requirements can differ between birthmothers and birthfathers. While nearly every state requires that birthmothers wait until after they deliver before they can sign a consent, many states now allow birthfathers to sign the consent at any time before the delivery. The rationale behind this is that sometimes birthfathers are available to sign a consent earlier in the pregnancy, whereas they may not easily be found after the birth of the baby. If a birthfather is willing to consent to an adoption, most states feel that it is important to give him that opportunity even before the birth of the baby. After all, birthfathers do not go through the same physical changes that birthmothers do after birth.

After the consent is signed, some states allow the birthparents to revoke it or change their minds about the adoption. In other words, if a birthparent decides he or she made the wrong decision in placing the baby for adoption, there is sometimes a window of opportunity for him or her to regain custody of the child.

The laws vary widely on this subject. For example, in some states, a consent signed by a birthmother 72 hours after the birth of the baby is considered to be irrevocable. In other words, the birthparents' rights are forever terminated. In other states, the signing of a consent is viewed as an indication of the birthparents' intent, but their parental rights may not be terminated until a hearing takes place months down the road. In the intervening time between the signing of the consent and the termination hearing, the birthparents have the right to change their minds.

In every adoption, there comes a point when birthparents can no longer change their minds. Whether it is upon the signing of the consent, when a judge signs an order terminating the parental rights of the birthparent after a hearing, or when the judge signs the final adoption decree, all states feel that there should be some finality, and security for the child, to make it impossible for a birthparent to defeat an adoption.

Requirements for Minor Birthparents

If a birthparent is considered a minor, some states have extra requirements about who must be notified. (Note that the definition of a minor varies from state to state as well: It can be someone who is anywhere from 16 to 21 years of age, with the most common definition of a minor being somebody who is younger than 18 years of age.) Many states require that if a birthparent is a minor, the birthparents' parents must be notified of a hearing that would terminate the parental rights of their minor child. Some states go one step further than sending a mere notice to the birthparents' parents: They require that the parents of a minor also consent to the adoption. More progressive states, however, no longer require the consent of a minor's parents.

A birthparent should notify his or her parents as soon as possible about his or her intention to place a baby for adoption, since the court will usually require this anyway. If a minor's parents disagree with their child's wish to place the baby for adoption, many courts will weigh the maturity and competency of the minor birthparent against the minor's parents' reasons for not allowing the adoption. One scenario in which a court might go against the wishes of a minor birthparent to place a child for adoption is if the minor parent's parent already is raising a sibling of the baby. Many courts do not wish to separate siblings if it can be helped.

Birthfathers

Many birthmothers wonder whether they have to inform a birthfather about their pregnancy and their desire to place a baby for adoption. Most states require that a birthfather be notified of an adoption. This is because the birthfather, by virtue of being biologically connected to the child, has rights to the baby, just as the birthmother does.

Even if the birthfather knew the birthmother for only one day and never supported her during the pregnancy or inquired about her welfare, he still has the right to know that he is the father of a baby and oppose an adoption, if he desires. Even birthfathers that are serving time in prison have rights to their children. Do not assume that a birthfather's rights will automatically be terminated just because he has had little contact with a birthmother or because he is not living a model life.

Many times, a birthmother will state that she knows the first and last name of a birthfather but not his current whereabouts. In those instances, a diligent attempt must be made to find the birthfather and notify him of the adoption. Many states have paternity registries that provide a birthfather with the opportunity to notify the state if he wishes to claim paternity to a child that he knows will be born or has been born. In some states, if a birthfather fails to register, he cannot be heard to assert any rights to a baby.

Even if a birthfather does not sign a consent, in most states, his parental rights can still be terminated. So long as he is not opposed to the adoption, he is not required to sign any documents in order for the adoption to move forward. Many birthfathers do not realize that by allowing their child to be placed for adoption, they are forever relieved of any child support obligations for that child. An adoption severs all rights a biological father has to his child—he is considered a legal stranger to his child once his parental rights have been terminated. By the same token, once the child has been legally adopted, the biological father does not have the right to visit with the child, unless, of course, the adoptive family entered into an open adoption agreement with him.

When a birthmother is married to a man who is not the biological father of the baby, he is often considered the legal father of the baby. Many states presume that if a baby is conceived while the birthmother is married, her husband must be the father, so those states require that the husband consent to the adoption. If he chooses not to consent, his rights must be terminated against his will for the adoption to occur.

Some birthmothers do not want their husbands to know about the adoption, perhaps because they have been separated from them for years and do not wish for them to know their personal business. Unless such a birthmother can produce a divorce decree, a long separation does not relieve the need to notify the legal father of the adoption. If the biological mother and father are willing to submit to DNA testing, proving that they are in fact the baby's parents and thereby ruling out the legal father as the actual father, it might not be necessary to notify the legal father. Whether or not this can be done depends on the willingness of the judge in the state before whom a birthparent will appear.

Reimbursement of Birthparent Expenses
The issue of whether adoptive parents can reimburse a birthparent for living expenses related to the pregnancy, birth and delivery of the baby also vary from state to state. Some states have

strict laws disallowing reimbursement of any expenses except for medical expenses of the baby or the birthmother during the pregnancy and delivery. Other states allow the adoptive family to reimburse a birthmother for such expenses as housing, food, maternity clothes, counseling and transportation.

States that allow adoptive parents to reimburse birthparents for these expenses usually require judicial approval. On the one hand, it is argued that reimbursement of these expenses can look like bribery or coercion. ("If you let me adopt your baby, I'll give you money to make your life easier.") On the other hand, many birthmothers face extreme financial hardship in deciding to continue an unwanted pregnancy. Some birthmothers cannot continue working and may have no way of obtaining clean, safe housing during the pregnancy without the help of an adoptive family.

Legal Aspects of Open Adoption

Most states allow open adoptions. As Sara mentioned in the prior chapter, what this means is that there is some level of contact between the birth family and the adoptive family. One of the most common types of open adoption is one in which the adoptive family agrees to send letters and pictures through their agency or attorney to the birthparents several times per year. In situations in which identifying information will be revealed about a birthparent or adoptive parent (such as if the adoptive parents consent to having the birthparents visit the child), the party whose information will be revealed has to consent to the release of the information.

Most states do not have provisions in their laws for what happens if an adoptive family fails to live up to their agreement to maintain some sort of open relationship with the birthparents. A dissatisfied birthparent could bring some kind of legal action against the adoptive family, but there is no guarantee that he or she would prevail. Most states look at adoption as the severing of one set of relationships (the birthparents to the child) and the establishment of another set of relationships (the adoptive parents to the child). However, in at least one state, there is a provision in the law for the birthparents to have recourse if an adoptive family fails to live up to their end of the bargain. However, the law states that even if there is a legal dispute on the issue of openness, it cannot interfere with the finality of the adoption itself.

When each state draws up its adoption laws, it seeks to balance the rights of all of the parties to the adoption. The parties to the adoption consist of the birthmother, the birthfather, the adoptive parents, the child and the grandparents of the child. Many times, the wishes of all of these parties do not coincide. When that happens, it is up to a judge to mediate any disagreements between the parties involved. The guiding principle is usually whatever is in the best interests of the child. Some states give more weight to the rights of birthparents, such as when there is a longer period of revocation or when birthparents can change their minds about the adoption. Other states attempt to give finality to an adoption more quickly, terminating the birthparents' rights early on in the adoption process. States also vary on how easy or difficult they make it for a birthfather to assert his parental rights if he objects to an adoption. Grandparents also have varying degrees of rights, depending on what state is involved.

Remember, this is just an overview of adoption law in most states. Because this overview cannot make specific reference to the laws of each state, if you are considering adoption, it important for you to consult with an adoption attorney in your state.[2]

SARA

As mentioned in an earlier chapter, most people think that adoption is not within their reach financially. It is true that it can cost a significant amount of money. However, it is also true that if God has put adoption on your heart, He will not allow money to stand in the way of you having the child He has chosen for you. Look at it as you would if you had a child who needed immediate medical care. Would you hesitate to do whatever you needed to do to get medical care for your child? No! So while it's important to be financially responsible, be sure not to limit God as to what He wants to do for you.

Although you cannot put a price on the life of a child, there are certain financial realities that accompany raising children. Whether you have biological or adopted children (or both), it is always wise to have a financial plan for the future of your family. This needs to be a realistic plan based on what you are able to earn and save, not a plan based on a hoped-for eventuality such as a raise or an inheritance.

It is important for you to establish a budget from the very beginning of the adoption process. It won't be helpful if you spend $25,000 to adopt a child but now have to get a second mortgage to raise that much money. Of course, part of the home study is an analysis of your financial situation. If you are seriously in debt, with few or no assets, you may not be approved for the adoption.

Some employers will reimburse their employees for certain adoption-related expenses. There are also some insurance plans that will allow for the payment of specified adoption expenses (remember also to notify your insurance company of a pending adoption so that they can add the child to your policy as soon as possible). The U.S. military will reimburse active-duty personnel for adoption expenses up to $2,000, although this does not take place until the adoption is made final. A number of foundations will also assist people interested in adoption (see the resources section at the end of this book). However, if you contact these foundations, make sure that you are clear about the qualifications and limits they maintain for their particular type of assistance.

These are details that you need to ask about before you adopt a child so that all the variables will be included in your financial plan. Explore every avenue you have available in the planning stages rather than waiting until the adoption presents itself and you realize you are $5,000 short. Know your limitations in every way.

The Federal Adoption Tax Credit (Hope Act for Children) allows a tax credit for expenses up to $10,000 in the year of the adoption. Note that unlike a tax deduction, which is an amount subtracted from your adjusted gross income before you calculate your taxes, a tax credit is an amount that is subtracted, dollar for dollar, from your federal income tax bill. You should keep this in mind as you make your financial plan, although obviously you will have to spend this money initially.

The financial circumstances are different if you adopt from your state through the foster-care system. There will be little or no expense in this type of situation.

While it may seem that the process of adoption is more about money than the child, unfortunately money is a very real and ever-present part of the world in which we live. Some people think that the more money they have, the easier it is to adopt a child. This would be true only from the standpoint of the fact that having more money would allow you to have more people working for you to find a child. Even the wealthiest people have to go through the same steps in the adoption process. Money does not shield anyone from the heartbreak of infertility or from the disappointment of not being chosen by a birthmother.

RUTH

I must reiterate how important it is to have a qualified, experienced adoption facilitator, whether you are working with an adoption agency, a private attorney or a facilitator such as Sara. The adoption facilitator needs to be excruciatingly thorough, professional and experienced in all aspects of the process. He or she also needs to be kind. Choose someone who has these qualities.

Remember, this person will be helping you with one of the most important decisions of your life, and he or she will need to be able to handle your raw emotions in a time of great vulnerability. They will walk you, step-by-step, through a maze of legalities, decisions and emotions. Don't just pick someone out of the phonebook or ask a friend of a friend. Do your homework. Get recommendations. Choose wisely and carefully.

I did not have to deal with the financial aspect of the adoption of Windsor's baby. Windsor's father, Ted, was generous and provided well for all of us. He negotiated with his health care provider to cover Windsor on his policy. He also negotiated with the adopting couple through Sara for any reimbursement of expenses.

We used a private attorney, recommended by Sara, who specializes in adoption law. Although he was professional, he was also thoughtful and kind. He did not ignore our emotions or the sensitivity of the situation.

When it came time for Windsor to sign the release papers, the adopting couple kept the baby in another room while Windsor, Sara, the lawyer and I went into the dining room. The papers were spread out on the table. As the lawyer gently but thoroughly explained what the papers meant, it sounded so cold. His efficient kindness buffered the harsh reality. Windsor looked at the papers and then turned to me. With tears streaming down her face, she begged me one more time to let her keep the baby. It was an emotional time, to say the least.

The lawyer was patient. Calm. He let us take our time. He was respectful. But he kept reminding us of our purpose. Quietly weeping, Windsor slowly turned and signed the documents.

Recommendations

Find an attorney who specializes in adoption.

Prepare a budget for the adoption.

Know your state laws regarding adoption.

Get counseling for yourselves and for the
birthmother, if she is willing.

Notes

1. The American Academy of Adoption Attorneys. http://www. adoption attorneys.org/ (accessed April 2006).
2. The material in this section was adapted from Ruth Graham and Sara Dormon, Ph.D., *I'm Pregnant . . . Now What?* (Ventura, CA: Regal Books, 2002), pp. 174-182.

CHAPTER 7

Buckle Up and Pray

He planned, in his purpose of love, that we should be adopted
as his own children through Jesus Christ.
EPHESIANS 1:5, *PHILLIPS*

SARA

The process of adoption is a lot like childbirth; you cannot fully understand it until you have experienced it. Adoption will touch you in every part of your life: emotionally, spiritually, psychologically, financially and relationally.

The best way to describe the emotional climate of adoption is that it is a roller-coaster ride. But you are not on this roller-coaster ride for fun and amusement. Rather, you are putting yourselves out there in a way that is unique and frightening. You are trying to sell yourselves without seeming too obvious. You want a child with your whole heart, and your emotions are easily affected by your circumstances.

As you experience your personal roller-coaster ride, most birthmothers will be experiencing their own roller-coaster ride as they carry their pregnancies to term and pursue their decision-making processes. Quite simply, there is no prior experience that can adequately prepare either a birthmother or prospective adoptive parents for the emotionally charged business of adoption.

It may happen that a birthmother will look at your profile and decide not to meet you. You will feel rejected. Most young women, after making the decision to place their child for adoption, change their minds about it. There is, however, a big difference between changing one's mind and changing the actual decision. As the birthmother vacillates back and forth, you will have to come along for the ride. Rest assured, the majority of young women who decide in favor of adoption and also go so far as to choose an adoptive family almost always follow through with their plan. This is particularly true in the case of young women who have ambitions, plans and goals for their future. They are more likely to make a decision for adoption and stick with it.

One young woman I was working with believed that she wanted to parent her child. But as time passed, she began to realize that between attending school and working to support herself and her child, she would never be able to see her child. She had come from a broken home in which her mother had tried to do too much by herself, and she realized that she did not want the same kind of life for her own child. So she selected a wonderful family. For the next few months, everything moved along smoothly. The adoptive couple was present at the birth of the baby, videotaping the child's entrance into this world.

The birthmother wanted to spend a couple of days with her daughter, and the adoptive parents agreed. However, when the time came for the adoptive couple to take the baby home, the birthmother was unable to let go of her child. This painful and heart-wrenching scene continued for nearly three hours. The adoptive couple sat patiently with her and tried to reassure her, but to no avail.

Late at night, I took the young woman back home, baby in tow. When we arrived, she said that she was too tired to change and feed her hungry baby, and she asked me to do it. I told her that if she was going to be the parent to this child, now was a good time to start. She looked at me through her red, swollen eyes and said, "Here, take her to them before I change my mind again." So at 2:00 A.M., the newborn girl was placed into the arms of her adoptive father—in a deserted parking lot.

God Is in Charge

Experience shows that when a birthmother begins to meet with prospective adoptive parents, there will be a moment when she will just know whether these individuals are the parents of her baby. There may have been a long list of things she wanted and wished for in adoptive parents, but her heart and gut will more likely tell her who God has chosen for her child than will her head.

One such young woman I worked with said that she just knew the minute she met the prospective parents of her child.

The birthfather did as well. The main reason she was so sure was because she could see herself in the people and saw them interacting with their children in the same way she had pictured herself interacting. She also saw qualities of her parents in the couple, which in this case was a very positive thing.

Let me interject here that for the birthmother to want to spend some time with her child is absolutely normal. And for the birthmother on seeing the baby to say, "I can't do it" (can't allow the baby to be adopted after all), is also perfectly normal. This is why counseling is so critical—it helps to remind the birthmother of why she decided on adoption in the first place. At the time of birth, her hormones and her heart will be in charge, not her brain. (This is why in most states there is a window of at least 24 hours before the birthmother is allowed to sign anything legally binding.)

To allow the birthmother that time with her child can be both a good and bad idea. The time allows her to become more attached to the child, but it also allows her to feel as though she has had an opportunity to get to know her own baby before handing the child over to someone else. The pain of relinquishment may be greater, but birthmothers are often willing to make that trade for time with their child.

I once worked with a young girl who was carrying a biracial child. She looked through profile after profile, but she just couldn't seem to find the "perfect" family. One day, in the course of a phone conversation with a friend who was living half way across the country, I mentioned that if she knew of anyone interested in adopting a biracial child to let me know. In turn, she mentioned it to her sister, whose husband was an ob-gyn in yet another state.

A few days later, as this woman was walking through her husband's office, she casually announced the request. Unbeknownst to her, one of her husband's midwives had been on a list for a year and a half, waiting for a child such as this one. You know the rest: They were in a car the next day to go meet the birthmother. Ten years later, the couple and the birthmother are still in touch through pictures and letters.

Watching stories such as these unfold convinces me beyond a shadow of a doubt that *God is the author and director of our lives. We have to believe that if God has put the idea of adoption into our hearts, He will bring it about in His time.* This is why it is so important for us to listen to Him and to the counsel of those involved with us as we make this journey.

Working in Tandem

Often, the woman is the first one to decide that adoption is going to be the best way for her and her husband to have a family. It doesn't seem to matter whether the infertility can be traced to the husband or the wife—men just seem to have a more difficult time moving toward adoption. Women usually have a greater need to nurture and therefore are more inclined to consider adoption as an acceptable way to have children. Men feel a greater need to have their own biological child, and this strongly defined outlook causes them to be a little slower to come around to the adoption option.

It is important that you consider adoption for the right reasons. The primary reason should be because you want to be obedient to what you hear God telling you to do. It is also important that you have dealt with the infertility issues before moving on to adoption. There is a grieving process that needs to take place whenever something is lost. In this case, the loss is your inability to have your own biological children. Like any loss, this can pull people together or push them apart.

Psychologically, the inability to have your own children is difficult for both the husband and the wife. Most people never even consider that this issue will be a possibility until it happens.

Having children is something that you just assume you will be able to do, unless you have been given a reason already to know you won't. So when the reality and heartbreak of infertility hits, it hurts deeply and profoundly.

The inability to have your own biological children can strike at the core of your identity. It can make you feel so desperate that you may make having a biological child your primary goal. I have seen couples spend so much time and money on in vitro fertilization that when their options ran out and it was time to consider adoption, that option had run out too—they found that they were financially unable to do it.

Again, if you are dealing with infertility, it is critical that you receive counseling. You need to be able to move into adoption from as healthy a place as possible. Know that adoption will bring out the best and the worst in you. Remember to come before the Lord every day for guidance and grace.

Spiritually, the single most important thing you can do as a couple is pray together. Prayer will cement your relationship as a couple and make it strong enough to walk through the steps of your decisions about having children. Financially, as I stated before, you should prepare a budget, with the understanding that if you believe that you can only spend $10,000 on an adoption and one comes your way that will cost $12,000, you *will* find the extra $2,000. With the different types of adoption, the costs can range from about $6,000 for a private adoption up to $35,000 for an international agency adoption. That is quite a range. Obviously, your research and preparation become that much more important. Read the fine print, ask questions as to where the money is going, and shop around before making a final decision on the type of adoption that you will pursue.

The adoption process may take a significant toll on your marriage. Having a child, whether by your own pregnancy or by adoption, will never stabilize a shaky relationship, and getting counseling during this time can only help. My advice is for you as a couple to pray together daily, truly seeking what God wants for you and for your family. Because one member of the pair will typically be more involved in the process (which can feel to the spouse as though there is a lot of pressure to make this adoption happen), be clear on what you expect of your spouse and make sure your reasons for adopting are sound—and shared.

No "One Size Fits All"

There is no perfect adoption process, and for every adoption a different set of circumstances will prevail. I can't say it often enough: The most important thing you can do is to believe that God is in charge and that the child you are meant to adopt will come to you in a miraculous way. Too often, we are so focused on receiving an answer to prayer that we aren't looking in the right direction and entirely miss the answer. Don't limit God, and don't put Him in a box.

I received a phone call recently. A young couple with whom I had been working had decided to expand the parameters of their adoption. They had increased their budget and decided that a child of mixed race would be acceptable. As they put it, "We don't want to limit God." Well, the truth is that we can't limit Him even if we want to. He can and will change our minds and hearts to conform to His. We only have to be available to hear His still, small voice guiding us. There are as many different situations as there are adoptions, so the best thing to do before you begin this journey is to have as few firmed-up expectations as possible. Trust your heart and know that if this is part of God's plan for your life, there will be a child for you.

A woman I once worked with who wanted to adopt had a dream about a particular baby whom she felt she was to adopt. She was already communicating with a birthmother and believed with all of her heart that this child was the one she was supposed to adopt. Unfortunately, the birthmother and her family did not share this same dream—the birthmother placed her baby with another family. Sometimes, the desire to have a child can be so consuming that what you think is God's perfect plan for your life is not His plan, but yours. Still, every no that you hear will bring you closer to a yes.

Keep this counterpart truth in view: People may step outside of God's will for their life, and there is nothing you will be able to do about it. This can occur on both sides of the adoption equation. I have actually had potential adoptive parents say no to a birthmother's interest in meeting them because they did not feel comfortable with the situation. The birthmother can choose only one family, which means that someone will be rejected. For the adoption to take place, both the birthmother and the adoptive parents have to be in total agreement.

RUTH

It cannot be overstated that the process of adoption is fraught with emotions on all sides. It is a roller-coaster ride: Up one minute with hope! Down the next with disappointment. Up again with joyful anticipation . . . it is stressful.

With all the uncertainties and difficulties you will face in waiting for a child, you will need something to stabilize you. Paul, in his letter to the Philippians, wrote, "The Lord is near. Be anxious for nothing, but in everything by prayers and supplication with thanksgiving let your requests be made known to God" (4:5-6, NASB).

I love the idea that it is the Lord's presence that removes anxiety, allowing us to talk to Him with thankfulness before we even see the answers. Practice being in His presence, talking with Him about what is on your heart. Make thanksgiving a habit—you can praise Him even when things seem hopeless. Praise Him for who He is. Praise Him for His attributes. Praise will lift your eyes off the circumstances and give you God's perspective.

During this time, there will be many details and people to pray for. You will probably be praying for yourself. While you are praying for yourself, please pray for the birthmother. Don't forget her, especially after you have taken her baby home—for then, she will need your prayers more than ever.

What can you pray for? What are some specifics? You can pray that the birthmother will grow spiritually through this experience and that she will have peace in her heart and mind. That doors of opportunity to begin again will open for her and that her family and friends will rally around her. That she will stabilize and begin to look forward to her future. That she will develop healthy relationships and make wise decisions.

Whatever you do, don't forget her.

Recommendations

Pray and seek God's will, not your own.
Pray for the mother of your child (even if
you don't know who she is).
Hire an adoption attorney.
Be patient, God is at work.

CHAPTER 8

The Wait Begins . . . and Ends

But they that wait upon the LORD shall renew their strength;
they shall mount up with wings as eagles; they shall run, and not
be weary; and they shall walk, and not faint.
ISAIAH 40:31, *KJV*

SARA

The single most difficult part of the adoption process is the wait. You will feel as if you will *never* hear the phone ring and hear someone say, "I would like you to be the parents of my child." As your agency and attorney work with you, at times the wait can seem endless. It is normal to get discouraged. You will have to consciously fight against discouragement.

Of course, there is no defined length of time for the adoption process because every situation is different. Some couples wait for a year or more to adopt. Some may never have the opportunity. On the other hand, there have been situations in which I have called potential parents at 10:00 A.M. to ask if they would like to be considered for the adoption of a particular child, and by 5:00 P.M. the same day, they were parents. I once called a family on a Friday afternoon and the baby, who had been in foster care, was in their home by 10:00 A.M. the next day. True, these are not the norm, but they serve as examples of just one more way in which God can work in your lives and in the life of your child. The best philosophy when it comes to adoption is to expect nothing, and then everything will be a gift.

Too often, potential parents try to manipulate and control the situation. This only serves to make them seem desperate. The last emotion that you want to communicate to a birthmother is desperation. A birthmother wants the parents of her child to be confident, stable, loving and patient. While she probably has never parented a child, a birthmother will more often than not look for the good qualities she sees in her own parents as she looks for parents for her unborn child. One young mother I worked with said that the reason she picked the family she did was because the adoptive father reminded her so much of her own father with whom she had a very good relationship.

As you continue your seemingly endless waiting period, you will probably begin to notice that every woman you know of childbearing age has suddenly become pregnant. Now, this will not be true in reality, but it will *seem* to become your reality. The same thing will happen when you are trying to get pregnant. Everywhere you look you will see what appear to be pregnant 12-year-old girls, as if it was the most normal thing in the world.

Be Proactive While You Wait

Being proactive during this waiting process is more than just a positive approach. After all, it might just be that the person you spoke to after church about your desire to adopt will be the connection between you and a birthmother.

I once worked with a couple that was reading our book on unplanned pregnancy, *I'm Pregnant . . . Now What?* Their teenage babysitter saw it and asked if she could borrow it for her friend who just found out that she was pregnant. We never know how God will choose to create forever families, but what we do know is that we have to be open to myriad possibilities and try to listen to Him.

For those of us who are not used to feeling out of control, this is very hard to do. We live in a society that tells us that if something is wrong, we should fix it. However, there are some things that are beyond our control, and having children is one of them. These are the types of situations that will serve to strengthen our faith. As the psalmist said, "Delight yourself in the LORD and he will give you the desires of your heart" (Ps. 37:4).

Many young women may see your profile before you and your spouse will have the opportunity to actually sit down face to face with one of them. When this finally occurs, you must know that your very presence communicates to the birthmother that you are already committed to raising her child if she chooses you. This face-to-face time is meant to be a time for you to see and decide if you like the way she looks, sounds or acts. If you have any concerns in this area, you should address these issues either with her, your agency or your attorney before the meeting. The last thing the birth-mother needs is to have gone through that arduous selection process only to hear you say that you are not interested. This young woman is offering her flesh and blood to you, which is a most unnatural act. To say no for any reason is like slapping her in the face. If you have any doubts about your level of comfort with a particular situation, I recommend that you *not* meet with the birthmother.

Most birthmothers will want to talk to prospective couples on the phone before they have an actual face-to-face meeting. If they like what they hear, they usually opt for a face-to-face meeting. This may require travel, so again, be sure that you are 100 percent comfortable with this birthmother before you actually meet her. Birthmothers will usually have a list of questions they will ask you—everything from your educational philosophy to questions about your extended family, religion and your plans for when the child would become part of your family.

Be Prepared While You Wait

One issue that you will need to be aware of (although it will not be equally important to all birthmothers) is the question of the working mother versus the stay-at-home mother. In my nearly 30 years of working with pregnant teens who were considering adoption, nearly all of them have wanted and expected the adoptive mother to stay at home with their child. The reasoning here is simple: Why would they release their child to someone who would put him or her in childcare? They could do that. These young, courageous women want to provide their child with a life better than what they are able to provide.

I understand that in some cases, it takes two incomes to survive in today's world. However, I also believe that if parents were willing to alter their lifestyles, a second income may not be as necessary as they think it is. This is not a popular belief, but I believe that it is an accurate one. If couples are willing to go through the grueling process of adoption, they should also be willing to give this longed-for child the love and attention he or she needs and deserves. Children benefit from having a mother or father at home when they get home from school. Spending their first few years in day care, while possibly a helpful socialization process, does not do much for the child's ability to bond with his or her parents.

I went back to work full-time when my youngest was nearly three years old. I hired a full-time housekeeper, Winnie, who arrived at our home before I left and was there when I returned from work. She took my son to nursery school, picked him up, and generally did things that freed up my time at home to be with my children. One day, my son was sleeping when I got home, and when he woke up, he asked me where Winnie had gone. When I told him that she had gone home, he began to cry and call out her name. At that moment, I knew that I needed to stay home with my children. Whatever financial sacrifice we would have to make for this to happen would just have to be made. I also realized that I was paying to work, because I needed to pay for clothing, meals out, transportation and house cleaning. Having me stay at home was not as much of a financial sacrifice as we expected.

One issue that I would like to address here is adoption by single women and adoption by homosexual couples. Ruth and I firmly believe that God intended for a family to consist of a mother, a father and children, Lord willing. While some young women are comfortable with the idea of releasing their babies for adoption by single women or homosexual couples, we believe that it is not in the long-term best interest of the child.

When the Wait Ends

When you do finally meet the birthmother, know that as nervous as you are, she is probably even more nervous. Her nervousness, however, is covered in an underlying sadness—a sadness that she will not be able to hide or articulate. I was with a birthmother when she met the first of several couples that she was considering as adoptive parents for her child. The meeting went well, but when we got into the car to drive home, she began to cry quietly. When I asked what was wrong, she said that meeting possible parents for her child brought the reality of the adoption into a whole new perspective . . . and it was a very painful place.

Other birthmothers are sure that adoption is the very best choice for their child. As painful as the process is, they approach choosing the parents who will adopt their child as an opportunity to give that child the best life possible. They see it as a way to take an active role in redeeming their "mistake." (Let me say emphatically that no child is a mistake—the unplanned pregnancy is a mistake, but God has created the child for a very special purpose.)

Whether you are able to develop a relationship with the birthmother will depend on several factors. One of these factors is geography—if you and the birthmother live in different states, it may be more difficult for you to form a relationship (of course, many relationships have started and been nurtured over the phone). Another factor is whether or not you will be comfortable in getting to know the birthmother as a friend. Some adoptive parents do, while others do not. This is another issue that you will need to discuss before the process begins. I recommend that you do not make the lack of a relationship a deal breaker, but you need to know what your comfort zone is because this person could be a part of your life forever should you adopt her child. If you do not desire any type of relationship, you might want to seriously consider international adoption. International adoptions tend to be more impersonal and have less ongoing emotion.

Once a birthmother has chosen you, your excitement will naturally be tempered by the underlying fear (lingering ever so quietly in the back of your mind) that she will change her mind and that you will leave the hospital empty-handed. The best way to prevent this from happening is to make sure that she receives intensive counseling. This can be done through a crisis pregnancy center, a therapist with experience in this area, or possibly through the adoption agency. If you are able and she is willing, you might consider offering to pay for the counseling if she is unable to afford it herself. It will be a good investment. The birthmother needs to feel that she has been given a choice and that she has chosen adoption because it is what is in the best interest of her child. I often tell birthmothers, "When you truly love someone, you want what is best for them, whether or not that includes you." The fact remains: There is nothing normal about forever giving your child into the arms of another woman.

First Kings 3:16-28 tells the story of a mother who was willing to give her child to another woman rather than see the baby cut in half. I believe the true nature of a mother is that of putting the needs of her children before her own. Anyone who has had children will tell you that if she had to make a choice between sacrificing her child's life or her own, there is no choice. Children are a gift from God, no matter how they come into our life. As parents, we need to be willing to do whatever we are called to do for them.

RUTH

When you are in a hurry, waiting is hard. Actually, waiting too often seems like a waste of time. We want to get on with the rest of our lives.

For the birthmother, there is the waiting to find out if her suspicions are correct: She is pregnant. There is the wait before she tells her boyfriend. There is the dreadful wait to tell her parents and the wait to know their reaction. There is the wait to find out the reaction of family, friends, faculty and church members. Then there is the wait for the baby to be born. So much waiting. And underlying all of it is a sense of dread.

On top of that, the birthmother will realize that she has to make some decisions that will change her from a passive waiter to an active decision-maker. She cannot put it off. For some, nine months seems like an eternity, but for others it goes like a flash. Usually it is a combination. Sometimes, time drags; sometimes, it goes fast.

But the inevitable will happen. The baby will be born. Then the adoptive couple will take the baby home to create a forever family. They will start a future together. There is celebration and joy—as there should be.

For the birthmother, all that she has been thinking about and planning for comes to an abrupt end. She has empty arms and serious questions about her future. There is no celebration— just emptiness. The baby she carried under her heart and in her heart is now only a memory. Her life has changed forever, and there is nothing to show for it. Those around her have no idea how she feels. They go on with their lives—while her life seems to have stopped. No one understands.

Now there is more waiting. Waiting for the heart to heal, for life to move on. There is grieving. And a broken heart.

I am not trying to be melodramatic here, but the truth is that the joy of the adoptive parents is the birthmother's heartache. That isn't wrong. It is just the way it is—two sides of the same coin.

All this waiting *can* be productive. It can be a time of preparation. You will never have this time again. Use it wisely to prepare your own heart. Keep a record of what you are feeling and thinking. Pour it all out on the pages of a journal. Write down quotes or poems that mean something to you. Some people find that writing out prayers is very meaningful.

Use this time to develop your spiritual side. Develop a habit that can help you for the rest of your life—such as reading the Scriptures. You might prefer to find an easy version to read. I like *THE MESSAGE*—it's like reading a novel! Listen for God's voice. He speaks to you through your mind. Talk back to God; make it a dialogue. Don't be afraid to tell Him what you are thinking and feeling, including your anger, frustrations, questions. He is your friend, and He knows what you are feeling. Write down Bible verses in your journal that speak to your heart and your condition.

Yes, this is a time for waiting. Make it a special time of preparation for the rest of your life.

Recommendations

Remember that patience really is a virtue.
Be proactive in the process.
Tell everyone you know that you want to adopt.
Trust in the Lord . . . He wants what is best
for you more than you do.

CHAPTER 9

And Baby Makes Three

God sets the lonely in families.

PSALM 68:6

You have been chosen. The baby is due in three months, and you are almost afraid to hope that this is actually going to happen. You are excited at the prospect of finally becoming a parent. Yet, as Ruth and I mentioned before, during this time you should never lose sight of the fact that your gain is a result of someone else's loss. It is coming at the cost of great pain and sacrifice.

Birthmothers leave the hospital with empty arms, an empty heart and an empty womb. They have made the ultimate sacrifice for their child and for you. Their gift to you is priceless. So, as you become adoptive parents, it is helpful to have a window into the experience as it is seen from the point of the birthmother. Here is what Ruth's daughter Windsor has to say about it, followed by the story of another young birthmother, Cherie.

WINDSOR'S STORY

I remember how I felt when I first met the adoptive couple, Rob and Joyce, to whom I was going to release my baby. I thought that Rob would be an awesome dad, but that Joyce was just going to be an average mom. It wasn't because she wasn't as good a person as her husband was. It was because, from my point of view, she was the "other woman." Joyce would rear my daughter, hold her, talk to her, listen to her secrets and love her up close. I was jealous and angry that this woman was going to be my daughter's mother. What had she done so right to be the chosen one? Somehow, I felt less qualified to be a mother if I admitted that she was fully able to be my daughter's mother. She could never be *me*, and I didn't want to believe that she could love my daughter as well as I could.

So I distanced myself from Joyce and didn't allow myself to get to know her beyond a certain point. I wanted to feel justified in not liking her. Actually, I maintained my distance and jealousy for years. It was a one-sided thing. The distance didn't exist because of her lack of effort, but mine. Ironically, I trusted her and liked her enough to give her the one thing that was most precious to me, but still in my mind she was the other woman.

After I had just given birth, I was still lying there when I saw Joyce going over to my baby. I wanted to yell, "Get the hell away from my daughter! Who do you think you are?" I didn't yell. But I watched her—she touched my daughter first, before I did. Probably her emotions couldn't be contained and she just had to touch her. But I felt she had just ruined my special moment. I was so angry that I wouldn't let her visit us again at the hospital. When I was discharged, I told everyone that she couldn't be near us, that this was my private time with my baby and she just needed to let us be alone. Other people thought this was cruel, and to some extent I knew that was true.

I tried to do the best thing in spite of the way I felt. When I walked into the house where Joyce and Rob were, I made a slow climb up the stairs with my baby in my arms. I knocked on the door with tears streaming down my face. When Joyce opened the door, she seemed surprised to see me standing there. I handed her the baby and said, "Here is your daughter." That simple action and those four words felt like a knife slicing through my heart and my soul. But I wanted my new daughter and her new mom to have special time together, too.

CHERIE'S STORY

Nancy, the adoptive mother of my son, came to the hospital to see us after he was born. She came into our room and asked if she could hold him. I just about threw up when I saw her hold him—especially when she put her pinky finger into his mouth. How dare she touch my baby? It made me so mad to see her holding him; I just wanted her to go away. I felt this was supposed to be *my* time with my baby, my family time with my boyfriend and baby and me. It was time for just the three of us, our little family—even if it was all a fairy tale—and it was so nice to be together.

Even though it was nearly impossible for me to let Nancy come into the room, I knew that she really needed to see the baby and bond with him right then, when he was still only a few hours old. I look back now and think, *Duh, this is the person that you are trusting to be this child's mother for the rest of his life, and you can't let her* hold *him?*

As hard as it is, birthmothers need to see the adoptive parents with the baby. After all, they are soon to be that child's parents. I know of other girls who have not allowed the adoptive mother to hold the baby, or who made a big stink over the whole thing. They should have realized that the adoptive parents need to be with the baby just as much as they do.

At the same time, I feel very strongly that the birthmother needs to spend some private time with her child. It's hard to know how much time is too much in terms of getting overly attached and making the process of letting go more difficult than it already is. There cannot be one set time that will be best for everyone. For me, it was very important that I got to spend time with my son and my boyfriend alone. It was also important to me that my parents spent time with the baby (their grandson) and that my siblings came to be with him as well.

My son was with me for several days before he could legally leave the state. I did not want to bring him home with me because it would have been harder to let him go, and because I would have had memories of him in the house and in my room. We had a ceremony the night he left. My family, my boyfriend's family and the adoptive parents were present. A minister prayed, and we all shared and passed the baby around. It was the hardest thing I have ever done, walking out that night without my son. But God got me through it, and I knew that this was the best decision for him. So what if my heart had been ripped out and I thought I would die? I did heal, and I am thankful that my son is alive and thriving in his home with his family.

I believe that it is important for a birthmother to name her baby, although she needs to accept the fact that the baby she gave birth to is now someone else's child, and they can name the baby whatever they please. We chose a few names and told the adoptive parents that we would be honored if they would even consider naming him one of the names we had chosen—either as a first or middle name. They chose a different first name for him, though, but there was nothing wrong with that. In the first year or so after he was born, it was hard to hear him called by the name they had given him, "Jesse." In my mind, he was "Isaiah." But in all the letters and conversations, his name was Jesse. After a little over a year, I began to accept what they had named him.

He answers to the name Jesse. He does not know the name I gave him at birth. Accepting that fact was a big step. I figured that I had better get over it and accept the fact that there was nothing I could do to change it. I think it also helped me to accept a little more that he is *their* son. He will always be my child, but they are his parents and he is their son. Our son.

SARA

When the day arrives for the child to become part of your family, there are several things that you will need to keep in mind.

First, if you already have other children (who most likely are young), you should have prepared them for the arrival of the new addition to the family. It doesn't really matter whether the baby is your biological child or adopted; either way, this baby represents someone who will be taking away some of their time with you. It will help your other children to be allowed to feel as much a part of the adoption process as possible. If you have the opportunity to meet the birthmother face to face, see if your other children can have this same opportunity. Having a complete family time like this will also help the birthmother, because she will be able to see how you already relate to children.

Second, to ensure that you will have an adoption experience that you can look back on with positive feelings, remember the following ingredients:

1. *Be sure that the Lord is at the center of your lives and at the center of the adoption experience.* Be sure that the adoption is His will for you and not just your own selfish desire to have a child. Most of the young women I have worked with over the years have been young Christian women, so they too were seeking God's direction for their lives and for the life of their child. What happens if you and the birthmother get different guidance from God? Of course, this can and does occur. This is where trusting the Lord in both your life and the life of any potential birthmother will really be put to the test. What you may think is best for a pregnant 14-year-old girl may not match with what God will speak to her if she listens to Him. Remember, if God has called you to adopt, He has already chosen the child you will parent. Just step aside and let Him lead the way.

2. *Seek and accept the counsel of friends while you are on this journey.* Know that God can and will use everyone and everything for His good purpose.

3. *Look at the bigger picture.* While not every young woman who chooses adoption is a Christian, as hard as it may be to relate to her on a spiritual level, God

may have given you this opportunity for more than merely having her child become part of your family. He may want to use you to bring her into His family.

I was counseling a young girl one day who had decided that adoption was what she wanted to do. I was new to the role of facilitator, but I knew about a few hopeful couples, so I got on the phone and asked for their profiles. One couple in particular struck me as a family that this girl was going to like, but I had already made a hard and fast rule to keep my opinions to myself. This couple provided what turned out to be a lengthy home study instead of a one-page profile. The birthmother took it, started reading it, and then suddenly declared, "I am not going to read all of that. Give me the next one." I did, but I really felt the Lord nudging me to have this couple provide this young woman with something shorter and more to the point to read. At our next meeting, the young woman asked for more profiles. This time, I had one from the same couple that was shorter and included a picture of them. She looked at it, read it and immediately said, "I want to meet them." This is the young woman I mentioned in chapter 5, the one who introduced the adoptive mother at the banquet as "the mother of my baby."

The lesson here is a simple one: Everyone involved in the situation needs to listen to the Lord, because He will speak to and guide everyone involved.

RUTH

The lovely young couple left with "our" baby in their arms. The car drove out of sight. My daughter wept with wrenching sobs, as any mother would who had just lost her firstborn.

In spite of the mood of the moment, I still felt sure that we had made the right choice. But I was not confident about what the future would hold for us now. As I have said, this was going to be a new normal. At that time, I could not foresee what that might look like, and I had to trust God for the unknown. For the immediate future, my concern was for my daughter, because she was emotionally and physically spent. (If you are interested, I have written about the events that occurred in the aftermath of the birth and adoption in *I'm Pregnant . . . Now What?*)

From time to time, people ask me if I regret the choice that my daughter made to release her baby for adoption. Emphatically, I say *no*! I am confident, as is my daughter, that what she did was best for the baby. That little girl is growing up in a wonderful family. They love her and are rearing her to love Jesus. In her family, she is developing her gifts and exploring her possibilities. What more could I want for my grandchild?

Are there times when I am sad? Yes, of course. There is an ache in my heart as I fill out the annual charity gift card in her name. I study her photo carefully each year at Christmas when it arrives in the mail. It sits beside my bed as a constant reminder to pray for her.

But I choose not to live in the "what could have beens." I choose to live in God's love, knowing that He is sovereign and full of grace. He has been in control all along—even when things were in chaos. He has loved us and He has given us grace to go through this situation and come out on the other side stronger and better. I have the pride and satisfaction in knowing that my daughter did the most loving, most courageous thing that any mother could do: She put her child first. She gave life to her baby and then made sure her daughter had the best that she could offer—even though that did not include her.

While we do not have direct contact with the baby or her parents, they are part of our family—we are simply not *in* it. In some ways, the release and adoption mean that our family will never be quite complete. My family does not look as I thought it would, but in the twenty-first century, that is not so unusual.

I remind myself of the uniqueness within God's family. It is richer for its wide variety. Each one of us has a unique story of grace and redemption, and many of our stories are still being written.

So it is with us. Our story is still being written. Since the difficult times surrounding the birth of her daughter, Windsor went on to finish college with honors and then earned licenses for both real estate and insurance in the state of Pennsylvania. She is a strong, beautiful woman. This past year, she met and married a fine young man. I am proud of her.

Recommendations

Pray for the birth family.

If you have children, begin to prepare them for a sibling.

Remember that your joy is someone else's loss.

Be faithful in sending letters and pictures.

CHAPTER 10

Adoption: From the Front Lines

*Go home to your family and tell them how much
the Lord has done for you.*

MARK 5:19

KEVIN GALLAGHER

My wife, Heather, and I have successfully adopted three children. The babies came from as far away as Chicago and as close as 10 miles from our home in Pennsylvania.

Now, people call us at least once a month to ask if we would tell them about adoption. There are so many people who want to be adoptive parents but don't know where to start looking for advice. We are glad to share what we have learned through our firsthand experience, because we don't want anyone to miss out on adopting a child.

Most prospective parents have a lot of misinformation about the process of adoption. Some folks think that waiting lists go on for years. Others expect a child to cost hundreds of thousands of dollars. Still others believe that the only way to find a child to adopt is to go to China, Korea, Russia or some other far-off land. Most would-be adoptive couples are overwhelmed by the enormity of the task, not to mention the risks involved. They get scared thinking about all the "what ifs." As a result, they too quickly give up their dream of having a family.

I used to believe some of the adoption myths. Several years ago, Heather and I were in the ranks of the uninitiated. For years, as we hoped to become pregnant, we didn't really want to know much about adoption. I can remember brushing off the idea, reasoning, *It costs too much money. Besides, where would we ever find a baby?*

It was only after determining that we probably weren't going to be able to conceive that we seriously considered adoption. After being hung up for a while on whether we could give up on being biological parents without exploring even more medical techniques, we decided to move forward toward our dream of having a family by giving up our dream of having a son or daughter who looked, sounded and acted like us.

Of course, we were also plagued by the other classic fears of adoptive parents: Will we really be able to love a child that is not biologically ours? What if the birthparents change their minds and try to reclaim the child? What if the child wants to meet his or her birthparents? What if we end up having both adopted and biological children?

Those concerns seemed never-ending, and they nearly overtook us. Ultimately, we just decided to take a leap of faith. We are overjoyed that we did! Family life is everything that we always dreamed it would be.

Trying to Make a Baby

Our story is typical. Heather and I married young and decided to put off having children to pursue our careers. When we started trying to have children in our mid-twenties, we found that it was not quite as easy as we had expected.

Infertility is indescribably difficult. We spent four years doing tests and procedures, but everything came down to what we called "the monthly disappointment." The process was dehumanizing, with nightly shots of fertility medication and numerous doctor appointments.

We never imagined that we would become regulars at the fertility clinic. The doctors, nurses and technicians all knew us on a first-name basis. We became almost like family, except that this was a family we really didn't want to be a part of. In the midst of our frustration, we tried to find humor in things, such as the size of the injection needles or the amount of sperm needed for samples. I remember one occasion when I rushed to make it to a doctor's office before another insemination attempt. As I walked through the door, the doctor seemed surprised to see me. He quipped, "I thought I told you that you didn't have to be here today." I responded, "Doc, if you're gonna get my wife pregnant, at least I'd like to be in the room!"

As Sara has mentioned, one pitfall on the trying-to-make-a-baby trail is the sudden realization that everyone around you is getting pregnant. Heather and I found this to be true as well—our college friends, cousins, other family members, business partners and church friends were suddenly *all* having babies. We babysat when people went on vacation, attended baptisms and arranged baby showers, all the while silently hoping it would someday be our turn.

Heather remembers standing in the checkout line of a supermarket and thinking terrible thoughts about a woman behind her just because she happened to be pregnant. *How come she can get pregnant and we can't? What's wrong with us?* The questions had no answers. It seemed so unfair. We began to question God and His plan for our life. Those were long years.

In retrospect, we see that the trials of infertility were simply part of God's preparation for us as parents. All of the despair, hope, frustration, joy, pain, anger, fear and love were worth something. Now we can appreciate the truth of the Scripture, "In all things God works for the good of those who love him" (Rom. 8:28).

Applying for Parenthood

There are many ways to adopt children. You can go overseas, or you can go to an adoption agency, a social care agency or an attorney. In our neighborhood, we have friends who have been to China twice to adopt children. For them, going to China was an adventure, and they loved it. We have another friend who went to Korea to adopt a child. A business associate of mine went to Russia and came back with three children. Another friend found his two children through an agency in Texas. We also have friends who put an ad in a newspaper and found their baby that way. These friends weren't wealthy, nor did they hire some fabulous attorney. None of them had prior knowledge of foreign countries or their adoption laws. They all just had a passion to be parents, so they started exploring.

In our case, we did a little homework on adoption. (See the resources section of this book for some good sources of information about adoption.) Then we decided to pursue an open adoption because we felt we wanted phone calls and personal meetings with the birth families.

When we first met Sara, we were right at the end of the infertility treatments. When she came to our home, the first thing she said to us was, "So, why haven't you tried in vitro fertilization?" That sort of threw us for a loop. I said to myself, *I thought this lady was coming here to talk about adoption.* Actually, Sara was. She just wanted to be sure that we were ready for what lay ahead, giving us our first little adoption test. Adoption isn't for everyone, and she was probing to see if we were having second thoughts. I'm glad she did that.

As our adoption journey began, we were faced with the challenge of writing the profile. As a prospective adoptive parent, you are trying to tell your life story to a person you don't know—on one short page. I think we did 50 drafts of that thing. You want to sound serious, but not desperate. You want to express your faith (we are Christians), but you don't want to be preachy. You want to say you have a nice home for the child, but you don't want to brag. You want to show that your marriage is great and that you really love each other, but you don't want to be too sappy or transparent.

You also need to include a picture of yourselves that conveys the right message. We decided to use a picture of ourselves that had been taken by a lake where we had recently vacationed. It showed the two of us dressed casually with smiles on our faces. We did not include pictures of our house, the family dog, the potential baby's room or the grandparents and cousins. Some people really want to show pictures of those things in the hope of revealing more about who they are. It makes sense. There's no right or wrong way to do your profile. Because the profile is for an open adoption, you can say more about yourself when you meet with the birth family.

I didn't really understand that at the time. It soon became obvious that Sara's idea of open adoption and mine were very different. For me, adoption meant we would let the birthparents know a little bit about who we were, unlike in the old days when nothing was known of the adopting parents. I felt this was somehow more mature and enlightened. We would exchange pictures, phone calls and maybe a few nice letters a few times a year. Never did I think that Sara would counsel us to meet the birthparents in person.

Before we knew it, Heather and I were on a plane to Chicago, working on our first baby budget and planning what we'd say at a meeting with a couple we'd never met. We met Christine and Jon at a restaurant in a suburban shopping mall, where we talked for about two hours. Christine's parents were also there, as well as a good friend of hers. In the beginning, it was intimidating. We were trying very hard not to say the wrong things. After all, these people were considering giving us their baby. Before long, the conversation flowed pretty naturally, with the women talking about the pregnancy and we men talking about sports.

Three months later, we were parents! When Dylan was born, we went back to Chicago to bring him home. It was almost like we were going back to visit family. Everything went well.

We were less intimidated by the process when we adopted our second child, Grace, a short time later. We met with Jennifer (Grace's birthmom) and her mother in an adoption agency office near our home. Jennifer was still coming to grips with placing Grace for adoption. Appropriately, she wore her emotions on her sleeve. We all made it through, but only with lots of hugs and tears. Grace came home with us two months later.

With Brynne, our third child, we were old pros. We met with her birthparents, Joy and Hank, at a local pizza place, and we wore jeans and sneakers. It felt almost like a double date. They were neat young people with whom we had a lot in common. It may sound odd, but we almost felt like a big brother and big sister to those two. Brynne was born about three months after our date with her birthparents (you can read Joy's account of this story in chapter 12).

The Question of Openness

Heather and I feel that open adoption affords all of the parties involved—adoptive parents, birthparents, birth grandparents, siblings and others—with an opportunity to better process their emotions. But even with open adoption, there are differing degrees of openness. All adoptive parents need to consider what level of openness they want before they make an agreement with the birthparents. With our children's birthparents, we enjoy varying degrees of openness.

All of the birthparents get periodic updates from us. It gives us great joy to write the annual letter about the children. We can reflect about the past year's events as well as dream about the future. Because of the letters, we have developed a habit we call "time stamping." Now when we are doing something particularly fun with our kids, we intentionally think of the birthparents. For example, one New Year's Eve we had a nice snowfall, so we built a bonfire in our backyard and invited a bunch of people over for sledding. The children made hot chocolate and S'mores around the campfire. We time stamped that experience and made a note of it so that we could share about it in our letters to the children's birthparents.

You might be thinking, *Don't you ever worry that you might have a problem in the future because of the level of openness you have with the birth families?* Honestly, we do not. Such fear is counterproductive. We feel that we are responsible to love each child unconditionally. If our children by the time they are 18 haven't felt loved and want to go back to their birthparents, it will only show that we have done a poor job as parents. In my opinion, our openness with the birth families reduces the likelihood of such an event, instead of heightening it.

Of course, there is the very real chance that our children will want to meet their birthparents in the future. As daunting as this might sound, it really should be no big deal. If our children want to meet their birthparents, we already have a foundation of trust built with them.

Jealous No More

I used to be jealous of couples that could have biological children, but now I think adoption is equally wonderful. Did you ever stop to think about all the things God has to arrange for an adoption? It amazes us how our children found their way to our home.

The night we received Brynne, we got a unique glimpse into God's kingdom. At our church, we gathered with our pastor, the birthmother, her family and friends, the birthfather, and some of his family. As you might imagine, there was a little bit of friction between these families and some anxiety in the air. Someone had brought a camera, and they started taking pictures. It started to feel almost like a wedding. Soon a time of prayer began, which went on for a long time. Then there were tears, laughter, times of sharing and healing. A situation that had caused so much concern and heartache was being redeemed. As our daughter Brynne was handed into our arms for the first time, everyone in the room was filled with joy. Surely God had orchestrated this adoption, as He had done with the previous two.

Recommendations

Know that if God has called you to adopt, He has a child for you.

Know that the journey may be difficult, but it will be worth it.

Trust the Lord and your heart to guide you.

Receive His gift of love and laughter.

CHAPTER 11

Adopted: God Chose Me and So Did You

Matthew Van Kirk

Increasingly, I have been thinking that maybe my experiences as an adopted child could help someone . . . someone thinking of adopting, someone thinking of putting a child up for adoption, someone who is adopted. I hope that telling my personal adoption story will help someone who is reading this.

I'll start from the beginning. I was born 27 years ago in Iowa. I know that I lived with a foster family for about three months. Then, one autumn day, a couple in Michigan received a phone call telling them that their baby son was due to arrive shortly and that they could come to pick him up. They arrived at an office building and filled out some paperwork. Then, they tell me, when their new bundle of joy was finally placed in their arms, I started to cry. It's a moment they'll never forget.

That was October 31, All Saints Day, or Halloween as it's more commonly known. Was I a trick or a treat? The jury may still be out on that one . . .

Apparently, for the first two years of my life, I did not sleep. I cried all night long, for which I am still apologizing to this day. I know that some day when I have children, whether adopted or biological, I will probably be faced with the same "joyful" experience. In preparation for that day, I can look back on what my parents did to help shape me into the man that I have become.

Our Family Is Formed

It feels as if I always knew that I was adopted, but at the same time I never really felt that I was. I'm sure it would be different for a child who had spent more time in the foster-care system. My parents have always simply been my parents. They laughed with me when I acted silly or told jokes. They were there to pick up the pieces when I was upset. They cried with me when I was hurting. They were at every football, baseball, swimming, cross country and track meet that they could make it to, cheering me on and encouraging me. And when I was bad, yes, they disciplined me, much to my dismay at the time. But the most important thing that they did, the one thing that influenced every action, the most important thing any parent can do—they loved me.

I will be the first to say that I have been blessed. God certainly has had His hand on my life from the very beginning, and He certainly knew where I needed to be and with whom.

My parents had been married for three or four years when they started trying to have a child. At the time, my mom was a preschool teacher and my father was an engineer working for an automotive company. Like many other couples, they struggled to have a child of their own. After several miscarriages, my parents felt that they were being called to seek other alternatives. They decided, after weighing the options available at the time and with a lot of prayer, to pursue a domestic adoption. They went through the application and screening process, and they were approved. They were then told that they would be notified when a baby became available.

Several years later, they received that phone call, and they received me with open arms and open hearts. From day one, I was their child. I know that they did their best. I also know that being a typical kid, I did my worst. But we loved each other. And that is what makes us a family, above all else.

Our Family Grows

I think I first started asking questions when I was about three. My mom and dad sat me down one day and told me that I was going to be getting a little sister. Over time, they read me children's books that were about adoption or adopted children. This got me asking questions, because I was an inquisitive little boy. They explained to me some of the concepts that I could begin to understand, such as how sometimes when a lady has a baby and isn't able to take care of it, she can give the baby to mommies and daddies who can take care of the child. They told me that God had a special plan for all of those babies because He made sure that the right babies went to the right people. They explained to me that they were not able to have a baby, so God gave me to them. Now, God was going to give them, and me, a little baby girl.

I was so excited. My mom and dad practiced with me how to change diapers, how to hold a baby, and how to feed a baby—all of the basics—so that when my sister did arrive, I would be able to interact with her even as a young child myself. I could not wait until we finally got my sister.

One day, we got the call. We piled in the car and went to pick up my sister. This delivery was a little bit different, though. This time, we didn't go to an office building. Instead, we went to the airport. For some reason, there was some sort of a strike with the airline workers, and in order to expedite the receiving process, we went directly to the airport. So there we were, me and my parents and some family friends, sitting in a private airport lounge together. I still remember what it looked like. Tall windows faced the airstrip. Right in front of the windows were wood benches with blue cushions. I remember that I could stand on them and look out at the planes as they took off, landed and taxied down the airstrip.

I was told several times to calm down and stop running from one end of the room to the other across this solid row of benches in front of the windows. I was very excited that my sister would be coming by airplane. I think a few jokes about the stork were made for my benefit. I probably fell for them and then started staring out the window looking for a large white bird flying overhead. It was dark, so if the stork didn't have any landing lights, I wasn't going to be able to see him.

Finally, there was a knock at the large paneled doors, and a man poked his head through. My parents stood up expectantly, and I jumped off the window benches and ran over next to them. I stood right beside my mom and dad, craning my little neck to see if there was anyone else outside the door. The man talked with my parents for a while, and I completely lost interest. I just wanted my sister.

After a while longer, there was another knock on the door. The entire room fell silent. The door cracked open just a little. Another man poked his head in the room, but this time there was a woman behind him. This woman had something in her hands that looked like a bundle of blankets. Again, I ran over to stand by my parents. The first man who had come into the room took the bundle from the woman and brought it to my parents. My mom held out her arms and took the blankets. My dad held me up and introduced me to my new baby sister.

All of a sudden, the tiny, tiny baby started to cry. I was in awe. How could this little bundle make so much noise? It was a taste of things to come. To this day, my sister is still the loud one in the family! My mom quickly figured out that she was crying for a reason: She had a dirty diaper. I, being the helpful older brother and wanting to see up close what exactly this little person was so upset about and to help right whatever wrong was befalling her, asked my parents if I could help change the diaper. My parents pulled up a chair so that I could stand and help them remove the offending garment. One look and whiff and I knew all too well why my new baby sister was in such a foul mood. I backed away and leaned against the back of the chair, still standing on the seat. "Mom," I said, "I'll let you take care of this one." Everyone in the room laughed.

From that point on, I was no longer looking out the windows at airplanes. Instead, I kept stealing glances at this precious little package that God had given to me and my parents.

This *was* a special package, just as my parents had promised. Once my sister had a clean diaper and had calmed down, we then sat down as a family, with my dad holding me, and my mom holding my sister. It was complete. The four of us were together, just as we were meant to be.

From that point on, my little sister was mine to protect. I was told to look out for her, to be gentle with her, and to be a good example for her. I would go into the nursery every morning and hang my head over the side of her crib. I would stare at her and she would wake up. I would let her grab my hand, and she would hold tight. I would lean in and give her a kiss on the forehead. And every morning, she would reach up and grab a fistful of my light blond hair and yank out a wad of it. I still tell my sister that I will hold her solely responsible if I go bald! My mother said I never made a sound. It's amazing what older siblings will put up with.

We were truly brother and sister.

Noticing Differences

As I entered school age, I began to better understand what it meant to be adopted. Until that point, it had never occurred to me that I looked different from the rest of my family. I was tall for my age, skinny, and had hair so blond it looked like it had been bleached. My Swedish, Norwegian and German background made me bear little resemblance to the other members of my family, who all had dark hair and ranked on the shorter end of the percentile chart.

The differences really became apparent when I started school. Both of my parents took a very active role early in my education, and since my mom had become a stay-at-home mom after we came along, she had time available during the school day to participate in classroom activities. Besides, she herself had a teaching degree. So she always volunteered, if possible, to be one of the class moms. With my mom coming to my classroom so often, other kids started noticing the differences between us and began asking me questions: "Why don't you look like your mom?" "Why does your mom have brown hair and you have blond?" "Why is your mom so short?"

At first, these sorts of questions bothered me. Why *didn't* I look like my mother? Why *was* I so different? I think it helped that another girl in my class was also adopted. The fact of her adoption was even more apparent than mine—she was Korean and her other family members were not.

When these questions began to bother me, I brought them to my parents. They had always told me that if I ever had a question about anything, I could always bring it to them. In this case, they simply reminded me that I was adopted and since I came from different people, I would look different. Once that sank in, I could answer my classmates' questions to a satisfactory degree. Being only five or six years old, none of us really had the attention span to dig into the subject very deeply.

Now that I'm older, my family always has a chuckle when people comment on my being 6' 1" and my mother being only 4' 9". It must be a sight to see me hug her. The funny thing now is that the same thing is starting to happen to me and my sister. We both happen to work for the same company, and even though we have been working together for more than four years, people still come to us surprised at the fact that we are brother and sister. She looks so Italian and I look very Swedish. We are seen together on a regular basis and are often referred to as brother and sister.

Growing Pains

I have to admit that I was not always a model child. Like every other child, I would get upset and frustrated when I didn't get my way. I would talk back to my parents and be smart with them sometimes. It wasn't right, and I was disciplined for it when it happened.

One time when I was older (not too old, mind you, because had I been wiser, I never would have dreamed of saying this), I was doing something that I wasn't supposed to be doing. My parents asked me not to do it, and then told me not to do it, and finally reprimanded me because I still hadn't listened. When my mother finished reprimanding me, I distinctly remember saying, "I don't have to listen to you, because you're not my mother!" I look back at this now and am shocked and appalled that I could ever have said anything like that to my mother. How much that must have hurt her!

Amazingly, immediately following that comment, she had the presence of mind to sit down and explain to me firmly that the term "mother" or "father" does not always have to mean the person who gave birth to you, but that it can mean the person who cares for you, protects you, looks out for you and loves you. She also added—and this comment has been reiterated since I was very young—"no matter how big or tall you get, I will always be your mother." It's true. She and my father have always been, and will continue to always be, Mom and Dad. No one else could ever take their place.

I haven't written much about my dad thus far, and I really don't want anyone to get the impression that my father didn't play a major role in my life. My dad has always been there for me, especially in the evening time after he came home from work and on the weekends. He worked very hard to provide for us, and I don't feel that should be overlooked. Since he wasn't able to be there during the morning and afternoon hours, when he got home he would spend as much time with me and my sister as possible.

In the summertime, Dad and I would go out in the yard and play catch every evening, tossing the ball back and forth. When I had some trouble with hitting the ball, he took me to the batting cages and gave me tips on how I could improve my swing to hit the ball harder and farther. My dad also used to let me help him mow the lawn. I would sit on his lap on the riding mower, and he would press the gas pedal while I steered the tractor. After I was old enough, I was able to mow the lawn myself. I think part of the reason I still enjoy mowing the lawn to this day is because I started out having such a great time doing it when I was little.

One area that I always struggled with in school was math. I hated math. I could do it in my homework, but whenever I would have to take a test, I would completely freeze up. My dad is an engineer. Math is his forte. He can do amazing things with equations and numbers, and he enjoys it.

I remember being in the third grade and beginning to learn the multiplication tables. $1 \times 1 = 1 \ldots 2 \times 2 = 4 \ldots 3 \times 3 = 9 \ldots$ Every day, our class would have a timed test on the set of numbers that we needed to learn for that week. I was terrible at them. I remember handing in my paper with only one of the answers written down, and I think it was wrong. When my dad found out, he worked with me until I was able to be the first one done and have all of the answers correct. We went over flashcards until I could say all the correct answers as soon as I saw the card.

I hated the flashcards and I hated the multiplication tables, but I did enjoy the fact that my dad took time out of his schedule to help me in the areas in which I needed it. This continued pretty much all the way through my final math class in college. Dad would spend his extra time going over math problems with me to make sure that I understood the concepts. He even took notes for me at the beginning of one of my college classes when I had enrolled in a summer program but my main out-of-town classes were not finished yet. I will never be able to fully thank him for his willingness to help and his dedication and devotion to helping me succeed in whatever way he could.

One time that I will never forget was when I was at an away track meet. It was just before the regular season started, and I had been training hard all year. For some reason, my parents weren't able to make it to this meet, but somehow that night my mom woke up from a sound sleep and knew something was wrong. She just knew.

What had actually happened was that as I was running my hurdle race, I broke five bones across the top of my right foot. Even though the bus had dropped us off back at our own school, I still had to drive myself home. Unfortunately, I had arrived at school later than usual that day, so instead of being able to park near where the bus would let us off, I ended up parking my stick-shift pickup truck on the other side of the building. It took me about 30 minutes to hobble around to my truck and begin the slow and painful process of driving myself home.

By the time I got home, it was around 1:30 A.M. I tried to walk into the house quietly, but my foot just couldn't take any more. I collapsed on the floor, with my running stuff strewn all around me. My parents heard the noise and came running down the stairs. I explained what had happened, and my dad then proceeded to pick me up and carry me in his arms up two flights of stairs to my room. That experience made me realize that no matter how old I get, no matter how strong and independent I may become, my mom and dad will always be there for me. I am so proud to call them my parents.

Spiritual Life

My dad also led our family spiritually. Every night after dinner, the four of us would sit around the table and read a Bible study together. Sometimes we studied a particular passage in the Bible and sometimes we read about Christian characteristics that we should all strive to develop. We would sit around the table and take turns reading, and each one of us had to give our input. (I think the study was designed so that we would always be paying attention, which seemed to work.) I remember thinking at the time that I just wanted to be done with dinner so that I could go out and play with my friends, but as I look at it now I see how beneficial it was to go through those studies. They helped to shape the lives of both me and my sister and show us the importance of having a family time every evening.

That family time in the evening lasted until I went to college. My mom always held dinner for my dad when he was in town. Even if he was running a little late coming home from work, Mom would always be sure that we all sat down together to have the evening meal. There was none of this everyone-eating-at-different-times thing. This was our time as a family to share what had gone on that day and how we felt about it. Sometimes I rebelled against it. I wouldn't share at all, or I would participate with the shortest and vaguest answers I could. Now I look back at it and can see that it was a great way to keep in touch with one another so that we knew how to pray for each other and encourage one another. I look forward to the day when I get to do it with my wife and children.

Need to Know

There is the inevitable moment in the life of every parent of an adoptee when the child that they have nurtured and cared for, worried over and prayed for wants more information about his or her birthparents. The child might be looking for extensive information, or maybe only a few tidbits. I imagine that this can be very difficult for parents. After all, your blood, sweat and tears went into raising that child, so why would he or she spurn you and want to locate another set of parents that he or she has never even met?

My parents were preemptive about this whole thing with me and my sister. When we became teenagers, Mom and Dad told both of us that if we wanted to find out more information about our birthparents, they would be there to help us. They knew it would be a stressful and emotional time, and they wanted to be there to support us through it.

For my part, however, I have thus far elected not to pursue finding out about my birthparents. We ended up having a conversation about it after I graduated from college. We were in my apartment, and the Barbara Walters adoption special was on the television. Mom asked me why I never seemed interested in finding out about my biological parents. I told her that I had them, that they are my parents, that I didn't need any more information, and that I didn't want her to feel as if I were looking for someone to replace her. She responded that when she signed on to adopt me and my sister, she always knew that there could be a day when we would want to know. She told me that she did not feel threatened and she would not feel hurt. She just expected it. I thought it was such an unselfish statement, and so honest.

It turned out to be true. When my sister decided to look for her biological mother, Mom and Dad were right there to support her through the research and eventual connection with her birthmother's family.

They also helped to support me through that time, because then for the first time it hit me—and hit me hard—that my sister had other people out there to whom she was related. I wasn't her only sibling. She had some half-sisters, she was an aunt, she was a niece, she was a granddaughter—to a whole different set of people. It ripped me apart. What if she ended up liking them better? What if I lost my sister? My little sister, the only sister I have ever known.

I'm still working through this one. My sister and I have talked a lot about it. She helped me realize that God always has a master plan, and while she has three half-sisters, she still only has one brother, and that is me. Besides, she still only has one father, since her biological father was not in the picture. And amazingly, she still only has one mother, since her biological mother died just three months before my sister first tried to contact her. It was reassuring to see that God really does plan our lives and will take care of us. He really does have our best interests at heart, and we can trust Him.

If you were adopted and feel that you're struggling with the whole idea (or if you are the parent of an adopted child who is struggling), you should know that it's okay to struggle. It's okay to raise questions. I can tell you that God has a plan for you even if you don't know what that plan is. He brought you into this world for His special purpose. He is going to take care of you.

At this point, I still don't feel ready to pursue finding my biological parents. I do eventually want to find out my medical history. I want to know what runs in the family. But I don't know if I will ever want to search out the woman who gave birth to me. Of course, I could very well change my mind some day. When and if I do, I will be very glad to know that my parents, my sister, and God are all standing beside me every step of the way.

CHAPTER 12

Birth Families Tell Their Stories

Joy's Story

I read in a magazine article about pregnancy that if you were going to the bathroom a lot, sleeping a lot, feeling nauseated, increasing or losing your appetite, or gaining or losing weight, then you might be pregnant. *No!* I thought to myself. *That won't happen to me. That only happens to other people. I just started having sex. Sure, we don't use birth control, but we're careful. Maybe . . . no . . . it just can't be.*

I kept putting it out of my mind until one night when I was at my friend's house. I told Brett that I was scared I was pregnant. She thought it was a false alarm. After all, I hadn't ever had morning sickness. I worked full-time and went to school full-time, so I must just be tired. But she suggested that we go and get a pregnancy test just to put my mind at ease.

We went to the store and got the generic test, the cheapest one available. Back at her house, the test registered positive. But what if it was wrong? I just didn't know what to do. I didn't want to involve my parents! They'd be so ashamed of me. I knew I'd really messed up.

The baby's father wasn't even my boyfriend. Hank was just a friend of mine. If I turned out to be pregnant, I'd have to deal with him, too! I thought maybe I could get an abortion. Or maybe I'd move to Ohio, get a job, have the baby and tell everyone later. Maybe I'd put the baby up for adoption secretly. I just didn't know.

For weeks, I continued trying to convince myself that it wasn't true, even though I did tell Hank that I might be pregnant and that he was the father. The pregnancy test just had to be wrong. But I felt like I was pregnant. I talked to a friend at work, and she said that she would find out how much an abortion would cost. She said she'd take me to get it done if I wanted. I started crying. *Is this for real? Am I going to abort a baby? Is there a baby? What a mess. How did I let this happen?*

In church one Sunday, a lady got up to talk. She was from a crisis clinic and spoke about unplanned pregnancies. *Great*, I thought. *Does my dad know something?* (He's the pastor of my church.) As she talked, I almost started to cry, but I couldn't make a scene in the front row at church. I took mental notes and then pushed everything under cover for another couple of weeks.

Finally, I had to know for sure if I was pregnant. I went to the crisis clinic to talk to a counselor. She was so sweet. She asked me several questions and gave me another pregnancy test. She confirmed my worst fears. I *was* pregnant. In fact, I was 13 or 14 weeks pregnant. I began to bawl. By this point, an abortion was out of the question, although in my heart I don't believe it was ever an option. I had to choose whether I was going to raise the baby or put it up for adoption. And now, I had to start telling people. I was terrified. This was it. The whole world would know about my sin!

I told Hank the news at a diner. He was glad that I wasn't going to have an abortion. I told my boss. She gave me a hug and let me know that she loved me and supported any decision I would make. Then I told my mom. I could hardly get the words past the lump in my throat. My whole body was trembling as I said, "I'm so sorry. Mommy, I'm pregnant." Much to my surprise, she just looked at me lovingly and gave me a hug. She said that she and Daddy knew that it was bound to happen to one of us four girls. I didn't think she would handle it that way. She didn't even cry.

After she told my dad, he left a rose and a letter on my desk at home. I started to cry the minute I saw it. In the letter, my dad told me that he will always love me. There was much more in the letter about his love, but also about his heartache. We had a family meeting later that week to tell my sisters the news.

My parents had a lot of questions: "How come you had sex?" "How many times?" "Did you have sex in our house?" "Why couldn't you wait?" I didn't want to answer those questions, but I felt I had to. I was the one who had messed up. We talked about adoption and parenting. They said that they would support me if I wanted to keep the baby, but they would not raise the baby for me. I understood and agreed. Then they went on to tell me that I was not allowed to hang out with any of those friends anymore. That made me angry. I felt that I needed my friends now more than ever. But I was living in my parents' house, and that was their new rule.

My dad put in a resignation at the church, although the church didn't accept it. I quit my job as a cheerleading coach at the Christian school my sisters attended. I wrote a letter to my church explaining my situation and asking them not to blame my family for my mistakes. A letter was also sent home to the parents at the school, explaining my situation. Talk about a public affair! This could not be dealt with quietly. Members of the church sent cards to me. People would come up to me and hug me, people I didn't even know. The whole time, I just wanted to be left alone. I was overwhelmed. I got depressed. All I seemed to do was go to work and school, deal with being pregnant, go home and sleep, and cry.

My parents wanted the family to go to counseling. I agreed that I would do it, but only if I got to pick a counselor that I somewhat liked. That was difficult. Finally, my dad told me about Sara and how she works with pregnant teenaged girls. He thought she'd be someone I could tolerate. I decided to give her a chance. I talked to Hank, and he agreed to go to counseling too. So we met with Sara. We were glad that she could help us find an adoptive couple privately instead of going through an adoption agency.

We started meeting fairly frequently to discuss all of our options. None of this was simple in the least. Hank wanted to raise the baby with me, and I wanted to release the baby for adoption. Every day was a struggle. Not only was I having to deal with a boy who wanted to marry me and raise the baby and live this "wonderful life" that I knew was fictitious, but I also had to worry about everyone else. I had to be careful about where I went, about everything I ate and drank (for the baby's sake), about Hank's feelings and my family's feelings—before I could even stop to think of myself.

Hank was upset with me for not wanting to raise the baby together, my sisters were upset with me for getting pregnant, and my mom was upset with me if I didn't do exactly what she thought was best. I kept trying not to say anything negative to people, because I was trying so hard to be perfect to make up for my previous mistakes. I didn't think I should contradict anybody.

The time came for Hank to make his decision whether he would agree with the adoption or fight me for the chance to parent. When a girl is pregnant, she has full rights to the baby—until it is born. After birth, the father and mother have equal rights. This meant that even though I was the one who was pregnant, the one who had decided not to abort, and the one who had decided that adoption was best, it didn't really matter what I wanted if Hank said no. All he had to do was oppose signing the papers and it wouldn't happen. We argued about it.

I didn't think Hank was ready to be a dad. He still lived at home and was struggling to hold down his job. And yet somehow, he thought he was ready to raise a child. I remember one day in counseling Sara asked Hank what he was going to do when he wanted to go out with his friends on weekends but he couldn't because of the baby. He said, "I can give up my weekends until the baby is grown!"

Sara responded, "And when's that?"

"You know, two or three years old."

Sara laughed. "Are you kidding me?" she said. "You're 22 years old, and you still live at home and your mom is still taking care of *you*! Raising a child is for life!" He just didn't get it.

Finally, after weeks and months of agonizing worry, stress and anger, he agreed to an adoption. Sara pulled some references from her files for us to look at. We were finally on our way to picking a family! Then Hank changed his mind again. He vacillated back and forth several more times, but we went ahead and met with a couple of families anyway.

As soon as I met the Gallaghers, I knew that they were the family (you can read Kevin Gallagher's side of the story in chapter 10). It was just a gut feeling. I fell in love with them. Hank really liked them, too. We asked Sara if we could arrange a second meeting with them and their two other adopted children. Sara set it up, and we went out with them to lunch.

When we saw how the Gallaghers interacted with their children, that settled it—we wanted them to raise Brynne. (They picked her name because I didn't learn her sex until she was born, and I didn't want her to have a different name after she was adopted.) Sara told the Gallaghers the news. Everyone was aware that Hank was still shaky about his decision.

Finally, the day came when I went to the hospital. Hank and Brett came, and so did Heather Gallagher. Brynne was born. After the 72-hour waiting period, we signed the adoption papers and had a ceremony with the adoptive parents, their pastor, Sara, my family, and Hank and Brett and their families. We prayed, cried and celebrated little Brynne's birth and her future with her new family.

When the time came for Hank and me to actually hand Brynne over to the Gallaghers, I had a weird feeling in my stomach. This was it, for life. We handed her over and cried again, but my tears were tears of joy.

My biggest hope for Brynne is that she will grow up knowing that I didn't abandon her. I released her because she deserves a family, not a potential divorce situation with her parents fighting and resenting each other and possibly her. I love her so much, and I know I did the right thing. I love receiving pictures of her. She is so beautiful and full of life.

JOY'S FATHER'S STORY

My wife, Giselle, had sensed that something was wrong, but even though we had a close relationship with our daughter Joy, I never dreamed that she was having premarital sex—or that she was pregnant. She was living at home, making good grades at a community college, observing her curfew, and informing us where she could be reached when she was out. She even continued to wear her promise ring—a ring worn as a pledge to remain pure. Many of her friends were involved with drugs, but Joy had convinced me that she could be around drug users without using drugs herself.

Joy told Giselle that after hearing the guest speaker on "Right to Life Sunday" at our church in which I serve as pastor, she had gone to the crisis pregnancy center. There, she found out that she was three months pregnant.

I went numb when Giselle told me the news. The words registered, but they wouldn't sink in. I decided to write Joy a letter in which I assured her that we both loved her and that we were thankful that she wasn't going to abort her baby. Yet I told her that there was no ignoring the sin of the situation, which she would have to face. I bought a single yellow rose and placed it with the letter for Joy to find.

We told Joy that we would support her in her decisions, but that we could not be expected to provide a home for her and her baby. She had been adamant from the outset that marriage to the boy who had fathered the baby was not an option. Early in the days after she found out she was pregnant, Joy decided that it would be a mistake to keep the baby. She felt that as a single mom, she couldn't provide a warm home environment or financial stability. Of course, we were sad to know that our first grandchild would be a stranger to us, but we both agreed with Joy's decision.

My biggest struggle during this time was questioning whether I had failed as a father. My wife also wondered whether she had failed as a mother. Why did Joy do this to us? Our love for her had not been destroyed, but all of our trust in her had vaporized in a few rotations of the earth. In particular, we wondered if Joy could be trusted to stop using drugs and to avoid her old friends. Because we have three other daughters, we especially wanted to keep drugs out of our home. This was a volatile subject.

Eventually, Joy chose to live primarily with a former church family whose daughter was her closest friend (and who was not involved with the drug group). We felt that provision of this sanctuary for her was a godsend, and we maintained frequent contact with her.

Joy's pregnancy threw my entire vocation into a time of uncertainty. Within a few days, we discovered that the scourge of drug usage among Joy's friends included other church families. Obviously, this was going to be more traumatic to the church than I had anticipated. I offered a letter of resignation accompanied by a letter of explanation and an apology that Joy had written voluntarily. The elders not only voted to refuse the letter of resignation but also to support Joy fully in the days ahead. They sent a letter of explanation to the members of the church along with copies of our two letters. By and large, the church handled the news well, although because of this issue (primarily the drug usage more than the matter of the pregnancy), some people left the congregation in the months ahead.

Sometimes, I think about what I could have done differently. The crisis center staff helped us with family counseling early in the process, and they were more than willing to do more. My entire family might have gained some perspective by accepting more counseling. We valued Sara Dormon's advice—and her resilience in the face of much turmoil.

Now, a few years down the road from the whole experience, one thing remains clear: God is working the situation out for the good of everyone involved. Giselle and I are very proud of how Joy has rebounded. Joy initiated some additional counseling, which helped her to resolve some lingering issues. She stayed in school and maintained a full-time job. She has made new friends, while showing discretion in keeping many of her former friends.

Our granddaughter, Brynne, enjoys a wonderful Christian home. Even though we have lost the chance to be part of our granddaughter's life—probably for all of our days, so we will always have that undercurrent of sadness—Joy shares with us the pictures of Brynne and information about her whenever she receives it.

MARY'S STORY

I was 14 years old, in the ninth grade and pregnant. I wasn't sure who the father of my baby was. I was also working for the first time in my life. My job was at a fast-food restaurant and I was making just $5.25 an hour before taxes, but I thought that it would be enough so that I could keep my baby. I was determined to manage on my own, even though I had no place to live and no support from anyone in my family. I was too young to sign a contract for an apartment, but no one was going to talk me out of keeping my child. I felt this child would love me unconditionally, as no one ever had before.

My counselor encouraged me to at least think about the possibility of providing my child with a two-parent, stable, financially secure home, but my pride and my love for this child were getting in the way. More to humor my mother and my counselor than to actually find a home for my child, I looked at profiles of couples who wanted to adopt. (To really look seriously would be admitting that I couldn't handle motherhood, and I wasn't ready for that yet.)

After a lot of talking and crying, I realized that my idea of life was just a fantasy. I decided to take a closer look at several couples. I liked two of them and wanted to meet them. I thought for sure that I would like one more than the other, but I found that I loved them both. Now I was faced with another hard decision: to which couple I should release my baby. After a few weeks, I finally decided on one of the couples, and they had a party for me. I met all of their siblings, their parents, all of my baby's future cousins, and everyone else who was special to them. Deep down inside, in spite of the heartbreak I still feel to this day, I knew that I had made the right decision for my child.

CHERIE'S STORY

I became pregnant when I was 17 years old. I was a senior in high school. The year that was supposed to be the best year of my life instead became the hardest year of my life up to that time.

From the beginning, I knew that I was going to go to college either way—whether or not I kept this baby—so I had to make two plans: one if I kept the baby, and one if I did not. There was no medical assistance available to pay my prenatal bills due to the fact that you have to be at least 18 to get welfare. So the bills were split between my parents and my boyfriend who was a college student with a part-time job. I had only a part-time job and no real money to speak of. I went ahead and applied to colleges, choosing schools that were close enough so that if I kept the baby, I would be within a reasonable distance to commute from home.

Once I turned 18, I was finally eligible for medical assistance and could get my prenatal visits paid for and receive other benefits. (By the way, just because welfare is free doesn't mean that it is easy to get or that it comes without a hassle.) With the help of my counselor, I planned out how I would be able to raise the baby. I went to daycare centers and checked prices. I went shopping and priced baby items—clothes, diapers, and so forth. I spoke with several other young mothers and tried to plan how I would be able to go to school, work part-time and still have time and energy to spend with my child. I also tried to find any type of housing that would be available to my child and me. In my town, this kind of housing was basically nonexistent.

My parents made a list of rules for me, including how many hours a week they would babysit, when I could have company, and how much they could help to support me. Even today when I look at this list, I still feel that it might have been a little strict, although I can now appreciate that my parents did it with the best interests of the baby in mind. I can also now appreciate how hard it must have been for them to sit down and actually write the list. They wanted me to keep the baby, but they also were not in the position for my mom to quit her job to raise my child. They were finished raising their children, and they felt very strongly that this was *my* child and therefore *my* responsibility. They were the grandparents, not the parents.

Finally, I realized that I would have to release my baby for adoption. I just couldn't manage everything alone. As I started the process of looking for an adoptive couple, I started with a list of qualities that I felt were most important to me and that I could not bend on. I looked at several profiles of prospective adoptive couples and met with several of them.

Of course, it was easy to find something wrong with each couple. Why? Because they were not me, and I felt that no one else could be as good a mother as I would be. I wanted to find flaws in every couple so that I could say, "Oh well, then, I guess I will have to keep my baby"—even though I knew that would not be the best decision for my child. Eventually, I had to realize that no couple could possibly have everything on my wish list.

It takes a lot of courage to be a birthmother who releases her baby for adoption. You have to make a decision to carry your baby to term in a world that offers you a legal and "easy" way out. Your choice will often be misunderstood by friends and family. Then you follow that decision with the ultimate gift— you release your baby into the arms of another woman. Why? Out of love and a desire to give your child a life and a future that you are not able to provide.

Recommendations

Be grateful for the gift you have been given.

Pray for the birthparents.

Love your child unconditionally.

Teach your child to love Jesus and that He

loves him or her.

Resources

INFERTILITY RESOURCES

Resolve (www.resolve.org)—A secular organization that networks local groups to lend support and information on miscarriage, infertility and adoption. Resolve sponsors a newsletter, conference, book lists and more. Contact Information: National Infertility Association, 7910 Woodmont Avenue, Bethesda, MD 20814. Phone: 301-652-8585. National Helpline: 888-623-0744.

Achieving Families **magazine (www.achievingfamilies.com)**— A magazine that provides informative stories and articles to guide people through fertility challenges. It is the only magazine written by infertility patients for infertility patients.

Conceive Magazine **(www.conceivemagazine.com)**—A magazine for women contemplating or actively trying to start or expand a family. *Conceive Magazine* focuses on all aspects of fertility, conception and adoption. Contact Information: *Conceive Magazine*, 622 East Washington, Suite 440, Orlando, FL 32801. Phone: 800-758-0770.

Hannah's Hope: Seeking God's Heart in the Midst of Infertility, Miscarriage, and Adoption, by Jennifer Saake (Colorado Springs, CO: NavPress, 2005)—Encouragement for couples dealing with infertility, miscarriage or failed adoption. This book is intended as a guide to assist couples in making wise decisions as they struggle through their grief.

ADOPTION AGENCIES

A Helping Hand (www.worldadoptions.org)—A nonprofit Christian organization dedicated to ministering to orphans around the world through adoption. A Helping Hand specializes in adoptions from China and Guatemala. Contact Information: A Helping Hand, 1510 Newtown Pike, Suite 146, Lexington, KY 40511. Phone: 800-525-0871.

Bethany Christian Services (www.bethany.org)—A family services agency that has more than 70 Christian adoption agencies and counseling centers across the country. Bethany handles a variety of adoption services, including networking, legal assistance and support materials. Contact Information: 901 Eastern Ave. NE, P.O. Box 294, Grand Rapids, MI 49501-0294. Phone: 800-BETHANY.

Holt International Children's Services (www.holtintl.org)—A Christian international adoption agency. Holt International is dedicated to seeing that every child has a loving Christian home. Contact Information: Holt International Children's Services, P.O. Box 2880, 1195 City View, Eugene, OR 97402. Phone: 541-687-2202.

Liberty Godparent Foundation (www.godparent.org)—An organization that maintains a 24-hour crisis pregnancy help line, operates a state-licensed maternity home and a state-licensed adoption agency, and provides information on beginning a crisis pregnancy help line. Contact Information: Liberty Godparent Foundation, 124 Liberty Mountain Drive, Lynchburg, VA 24502. Phone: 434-845-3466.

Love Basket, Inc. (www.lovebasket.org)—A nondenominational Christian adoption agency for domestic and international adoption. Contact Information: Love Basket, Inc., 10306 Highway 21, Hillsboro, MO 63050. Phone: 636-797-4100; 636-797-4100.

BOOKS ON ADOPTION

A Love Like No Other: Stories from Adoptive Parents, edited by Pamela Kruger and Jill Smolowe (New York: Riverhead Books, 2005)—A collection of adoption stories from parents who have done it. Tells the highs and lows of the adoption journey.

A Treasury of Adoption Miracles, by Karen Kingsbury (Nashville, TN: WarnerFaith, 2005)—Twelve short stories about birthparents, adoptive families, adopted people and the miracle that inhabits every experience.

Adoption Nation: How the Adoption Revolution Is Transforming America, by Adam Pertman (New York: Basic Books, 2001)—An award-winning book loaded with statistics and information on adoption.

Meditations for Adoptive Parents, by Vernell Klassen Miller and Esther Rose Graber (Scottdale, PA: Herald Press, 1992)—The perfect gift for adoptive parents. Using her family experiences, Vernell Klassen Miller includes theories about bonding to infants and older children, the stages of relinquishment and adoption, the process of entitlement, and the advantages of the adoption process.

The Spirit of Adoption: At Home in God's Family, by Jeanne Stevenson Moessner (London, England: Westminster John Knox Press, 2003)—The "how to" and "why to" of adoption. Written with a focus on God as our adopter.

Tell Me Again About the Night I Was Born, by Jamie Lee Curtis (New York: HarperCollins, 1996)—A heartwarming story about the birth of a child and the family who adopted her.

Twenty Life-Transforming Choices Adoptees Need to Make, by Sherrie Eldridge (Colorado Springs, CO: Pinon Press, 2003)—A book for and by adoptees that helps to begin the healing process by engaging the difficult questions and emphasizing adoptees' ability to take control of their emotions surrounding the issue of adoption.

Twenty Things Adopted Kids Wish Their Adoptive Parents Knew, by Sherrie Eldridge (New York: Dell Publishing, 1999)—An excellent guide to the complex emotions that are present within the adopted child and the adoptive home.

The Whole Life Adoption Book: Realistic Advice for Building a Healthy Adoptive Family, by Jayne E. Schooler (Colorado Springs, CO: NavPress, 1993)—A book that discusses issues such as what to consider before you adopt, how to tell a child he or she is adopted, how to help a child deal with memories of the past, how to understand the issues and behaviors that can surface in adolescence, and how to respond when a child wants to search for his or her biological parents. It offers hope and direction to those considering adoption and those desiring to improve the adoptive family relationships at any stage. For both counselors and counselees.

ADOPTION WEBSITES

There are an almost unlimited number of websites that address the issues surrounding adoption. The following list is by no means exhaustive, but the websites listed here are the most extensive and helpful. They are not exclusively Christian.

123Adoption.com—An adoption search engine.

Adoption.com—Provides information on all facets of domestic and international adoption, pregnancy and foster care. This website has a link to many others sites, all of which will be helpful to young women considering adoption as well as parents who are seeking to adopt.

Adoption.org—A search engine for 400,000-plus pages of adoption information.

Parentprofiles.com—A website in which those who wish to adopt can place their profile and have it accessible to many birthmothers.

Pro-Life Organizations

Birthright International (www.birthright.org)—Offers the same type of help that you will find on Care Net (see below). This organization has been around since 1968.

Care Net (www.care-net.org)—An accessible and effective abortion alternative organization, daughter ministry of the Christian Action Council. Care Net trains individuals, churches and staff of pregnancy-care centers to provide practical care to women in crisis pregnancies. This organization produces educational materials, sponsors an annual conference, and publishes a national newsletter. Contact Information: 109 Carpenter Drive, Suite 100, Sterling, VA 20164. Phone: 703-478-5661.

Catholic Charities (www.catholiccharitiesusa.org)—A ministry of the Catholic Church that provides services to women in unplanned pregnancies. Contact Information: Catholic Charities USA, 1731 King Street, Alexandria, VA 22314. Phone: 800-CARE-002.

Heartbeat International (www.heartbeatinternational.org)—
An interdenominational association of life-affirming pregnancy
resource centers, medical clinics, maternity homes and nonprofit adoption agencies. Contact Information: 665 E. Dublin-
Granville Road, Suite 440, Columbus, OH 43229. Phone: 888-
550-7577.

Hunter's Chosen Child (www.hunterschosenchild.com)—
A foundation to aid those who are facing the challenges of unplanned pregnancy.

**National Association of Christian Child and Family Agencies
(www.naccfa.org)**—An association that addresses issues of the
family and the child from a Christ perspective. Contact
Information: P.O. Box 307, Gridley, IL 61744. Phone: 309-747-4517.

Option Line (www.pregnancycenters.org)—A website that will
help you find someone to answer your questions immediately.
Consultants are available at all times. Phone: 800-395-HELP.

About the Authors

RUTH GRAHAM

Born in 1950, Ruth is the co-author of *I'm Pregnant . . . Now What?* and author of *In Every Pew Sits a Broken Heart, Legacy of Love* and *Legacy of Faith*. Ruth is the third child of evangelist Billy Graham and his wife, Ruth. Ruth is a published author and national speaker. Currently, she is speaking to women on real-life issues at Ruth Graham and Friends conferences around the United States (www.ruthgrahamandfriends.com).

For 11 years, Ruth served as acquisitions editor for HarperCollins San Francisco. For five years, she was the donor relations coordinator for Samaritan's Purse International, and then took the position of major gifts officer at Mary Baldwin College. Ruth went back to school at 40 and received a degree in religion/communications from Mary Baldwin College in 2000.

Because of her own teenaged daughter's two pregnancies, Ruth has a heart for young women who face the choices of an unplanned pregnancy. She is open about her experience with her daughter and talks honestly about their choices and struggles. She is an effective and experienced communicator. For many years, Ruth has traveled the country sharing her experience as a source of information and encouragement. Ruth is currently on the board of Birthmothers®, a nonprofit, parachurch organization that provides confidential, non-judgmental assistance to any woman facing an unplanned pregnancy.

Ruth is the mother of three grown children and grandmother of three. She lives in the Shenandoah Valley of Virginia.

Sara R. Dormon, Ph.D.

Sara Dormon is a clinical psychologist specializing in issues surrounding women and crisis pregnancies. For the past 25 years, she has worked with young women and their families as they faced an unplanned pregnancy and the choices this situation brings. Her own personal journey has given her this passion and desire to help these young women. She and her family have taken many young women into their home, and she has counseled them through the process. Whether they choose adoption or parenting, she helps them plan and prepare for their choice.

She has been a board member and counselor at the Amnion Crisis Pregnancy Center in Bryn Mawr, Pennsylvania, and has done extensive postabortion counseling. She has done television and radio interviews covering the issues of teen pregnancy, abortion and adoption. Until recently, she had a private practice in Lansdowne, Pennsylvania. Sara is an experienced and humorous speaker who brings a refreshing and honest look at some very difficult issues.

Sara is the mother of three sons and the grandmother to three girls. She lives in a suburb of Philadelphia with her husband, Bill.

Contact toll free: 888-800-4440
E-mail: sara@forpregnancyhelp.com

More Books That Offer Inspiration and Encouragement